"Where do I even start? I met Kevin maybe twelve years ago, and I became one of his consulting clients about nine years ago. All I can say is I have never encountered anyone with the ability to take simple business practices and dumb them down as simply as Kevin does. Once we talk, I always say, 'Now, why couldn't I see that?' He has become our only source of advice in our highly competitive company. If you ever have the chance to work with him, do not hesitate."

—James Buchannon
COO of a Large Brick-and-Mortar Retail Company

"Kevin helped me take my idea and turn it into a seven-figure business in three short years. I don't know anyone more clever, and certainly no one more tactical, than Kevin. I owe my entire livelihood to his expertise."

—Madeline Sinofsky
CEO of an Online Education Company

"We went from six clients and four staff members to 132 clients and thirty-one staff members in five years using Kevin's unique ability to show us the holes in our business and how to overcome them."

—Janice Garcia
COO of an Interior Design Firm

THE POWER OF
LEADERSHIP

WITH KEVIN GOODNIGHT

ALSO FEATURING
OTHER TOP AUTHORS

© 2022 Success Publishing

Success Publishing, LLC
P.O. Box 703536
Dallas, Texas 75370 USA

questions@mattmorris.com

Table of Contents

CHAPTER 1

Setting Goals And Relentlessly Pursuing Them

By Kevin Goodnight

Knowing exactly what you want to achieve and how long it'll take to manifest that achievement is crucial. According to Edwin Locke's famous goal-setting theory, goals that are more challenging and specific are more likely to be achieved. So, you need to think big!

Part of setting your goals also involves knowing what you want, and with that clarity comes herculean efforts coupled with laser focus.

Setting your goals is one of the most effective ways to enhance your self-confidence and seek meaning in your life. It'll move you to take action. And seeing this action will only motivate you further.

However, you may pursue a goal only to discover that it was never meant for you. While this may be disheartening, what you learn on the journey is never a waste.

For example, let's look at the story of Martha. Martha was obsessed with buying her new home and spent several months renovating it. But when she actually moved in, her enthusiasm dropped. She realized that it was the renovation that was actually exciting for her, and this realization enticed her to take a different career path. Today, she's a successful interior decorator.

As Martha's story spells out, her heart's true desire was to actually become an interior decorator. The house was a major component of her realizing that, but it wasn't the end goal. So, dig down deep and discover your true goals to enjoy your maximum happiness from them.

Avoid setting vague goals like being a "good" writer. Be specific! Instead, decide that you want to become a best-selling science fiction author. Instead of deciding to make "a lot" of money, commit to a specific salary figure as the goal to pursue. Instead of saying that you want to get married, determine the qualities your ideal mate will possess.

You should measure your goals in time (how long they will take to achieve) and quantity (how much). For example, if you want to quit smoking by cutting down your cigarette intake, then give yourself a timeline at the end of which you're down to smoking zero cigarettes a day. Your brain needs clear instructions to know where to begin. Giving your mind a clear direction keeps you from procrastinating.

Begin by taking a step back and taking an eagle's view of your life. Next, decide on your long-term goals. Finally, you break these goals down into easily achievable tasks.

To clarify this, let's take the example of Barbara. Her life goal is to be a famous novelist. She broke this goal down into the following achievable tasks:

- Read books that connect with what she wants to write
- Writing a daily journal
- Writing one page
- Attend creative writing workshops to assess her work
- Take a course in fiction writing at an acclaimed university
- Finishing her manuscript
- Scouting for agents and publishers

Chances are that you'll have more than one life goal. Apart from her art goal, Barbara needs to look at various aspects of her life and achieve the goals therein.

If you want to achieve your goals, they need to be *your own* idea. Chase the dreams of *your* heart—not those of others. Let's say you want to shed weight because your partner wants you to—and you're comfortable with your body—you're very unlikely to achieve that goal.

Determine if you have the ability—or gain the necessary skills—to achieve your goals. Take into account any limitations that could prolong your goals or force you to make adjustments along the way.

Let's take an example. Ralph has a chronic respiratory challenge that demands frequent hospital care. Since he doesn't have access to hospital facilities out at sea, this will likely prevent him from achieving his goal of sailing around the world.

If you've given yourself ten years to achieve some large goals, divide that time frame into increments to achieve smaller goals that lead up to your large goal.

Next, set three plans of varying durations: one year, six months, and one month. Figure out what you wish to achieve in these time frames.

Let's break this down with the example of Barbara. Barbara can set reasonable time frames for tasks that'll aid her in finishing her manuscript. Perhaps she'd give herself a month to plan out her novel and another one to write every chapter. When she's done with her initial writing, she might give herself three months of revision time and another six to look for a publisher.

Manage your tasks according to your goals and around time frames that work for you! Doing this will set you up with a reasonable expectation of the time it'll take you to achieve every goal. Fix your timeline as necessary to overcome obstacles along the way as you pursue your goal, but always have the big picture, with your ultimate success, in mind.

Next, decide on the things you'll do each day to achieve your smaller goals. Barbara will write a page every day. She'll fill in her journal every week. If you stick to your daily routine, you'll remain motivated.

Once you've divided your lifetime goals into smaller ones, you may find yourself feeling overwhelmed. You simply need to prioritize your intermediate goals and keep them practical and achievable. Writing down your goals helps clarify them and reminds you of them when life is trying to distract you.

Your life will be much more exciting once you've set your goals. Every little goal reached will boost your self-confidence and your enjoyment of life. You'll banish boredom because there's always something to do and a pot of gold to look forward to at the end of your rainbow.

The following questions will help you begin the process of goal setting. Answer them honestly:

- How balanced is your life?
- Do you constantly encounter extremes in circumstances?
- How can you balance your life and schedule time each day to work toward your goal?
- Do you have a sense of purpose?
- What are your most important core values?
- What matters most to you?
- What goals can you set that support this purpose?
- Are your thought and behavior patterns getting in the way of a happy, successful life?

Once you have some answers, you can ask yourself which areas need the most work. Jot down the benefits of your goal along with the challenges you're likely to face on your journey of self-development.

Flow with your life's challenges so you can sync with the universal flow. As you grow older and change, so do your priorities. Your older goals may not be as relevant today. So, it's good to review your goals from time to time. Prioritize the ones most important to you now, and place yourself in control of any upcoming changes.

Answering these questions with honesty will help you set your most meaningful goals.

- What does success mean to you?
- Is success the same as receiving material goals, having good relationships, or attaining spiritual awareness?
- What life do you visualize after completing your goals?
- How does your definition of success affect you and the people close to you?

Every action you take today helps to create your future. So, ask yourself if any of your habits could potentially hinder reaching your goals. For instance, you may dream about retiring early and running a luxury spa in a beautiful location. But if you lack the habit of keeping account of your daily expenses, you may find it challenging to save money and realize your goal.

Writing down your goal and regularly visualizing the outcome will help you focus on them. It's a proven technique that turns dreams into reality.

For example, you could write, "I am making and saving enough money so I can retire early and open a spa in a beautiful location."

Then think of an image that goes with this goal—maybe a scenic countryside is the perfect location for your spa. Or maybe the vision that motivates you is having a chocolate massage in your spa. How does it feel? Enjoy the moment with all your senses.

This exercise can also help you think of all those smaller goals that will create your lifetime goal. Fill in the important details. How much money will you need? How will you attain those funds? What can you do each day to achieve your current tasks that propel you toward this goal?

Figure out how you can make your goal easier to achieve. While some sacrifice will be involved, your overall journey should be a pleasure as you look forward to attaining your dreams.

Reward yourself along the way to boost your enthusiasm. Even telling a supportive friend about a small achievement provides a sweet reward in the pride you feel. Maybe you could even chart your progress on a sheet of paper and look at it daily.

If other people are involved in the achievement of your goal, or if it's going to affect them, tell them about it so they may support you in your endeavors. If you need their help in any way, let them know.

Sometimes your family and friends find it difficult to comprehend why you are so determined to reach your goals. While they may mean well, they could be struggling with their own goals. This could manifest in words and actions you may find discouraging. Jealousy is another possibility. Just be aware of these realities, and keep a positive outlook on your journey.

Be prepared to stand on your feet and rely on yourself instead of your loved ones for support.

It's understandable that you want to achieve your goals as quickly as possible, but patience and persistence are what win the day. Taking small steps and building on each small victory leads to more lasting changes.

- You'll have time for the other important things in your life.
- You can change course or make adjustments on the way if something unexpected turns up or if things go differently than you envisioned.

- You'll enjoy your journey because you'll have the time to pause and celebrate your small achievements.
- You're more likely to be stress-free by putting less pressure on yourself.

You're a hero! You set out to achieve something important to you, and you already possess the integrity and courage to see it through. On your heroic journey, you just might find yourself going off-track once in a while. That's completely normal.

Maybe you'll feel disheartened when tested (like all heroes are). During such times, remember that all happy and successful people have goals and challenges. You deserve to lead the life you've dreamed of.

Review your progress at every milestone to keep yourself motivated. Instead of allowing setbacks to derail you, allow them to correct your course. Allow small victories to propel you forward to the future you deserve.

Another way to ensure you reach your goals is to avoid situations where you're likely to give in to temptation. Let's say you want to drop some pounds so you can get into a favorite outfit for a certain occasion. You could find yourself returning to old habits, like diving into a calorie-packed pastry every morning.

You know that eating healthy and exercising every day are the paths to your goal, so find ways to build in support so you avoid temptation. Maybe you could get someone to remind you to get up early each morning and take an alternate route that steers you away from the bakery.

This is how most successful people achieve their goals. They avoid situations that would lead them to temptation. If you do give in, get back on track without self-recrimination and, instead, be determined to make a better choice next time.

Steve Garvey, former Major League Baseball first baseman, said, "You have to set goals that are almost out of reach. If you set a goal that is attainable without much work or thought, you are stuck with something below your true talent and potential."[1]

Setting big, complex goals is a powerful way to ensure you always keep your goals in sight and attain them. Consider the inspiring example of Melanie, a seeker of enlightenment. Ever since Melanie came across the most peaceful and happy individual she had ever seen (a Buddhist nun in the Po Lin Monastery near Hong Kong), she set a big lifetime goal for herself. She vowed she would work towards enlightenment.

On her return home to America, she joined a group of Buddhist practitioners and began to shed the unwanted skins around her (like peeling an onion). Over her ten years of practice, she achieved smaller goals that would lead to her big goal. In an attempt to purify her mind and body, she did the following things:

- Within the first two months of her practice, she became a vegetarian.
- In the next year, she stopped smoking cigarettes.
- In the next two years, she released the need for partying and rowdiness.
- After about four years of being on the path, she found she had transformed her lifestyle, ensuring more tranquility.

Melanie learned to stop blaming others for the difficulties she faced. Through her experiences, she came to believe in what her spiritual mentors told her. She created her own world. As she progressed, they encouraged her to find the answers to important spiritual questions within her without depending on mentors.

---

1   Harvey March 4 and Elizabeth Frederick March 5, "Let's Talk Sales! Inspirational Quote from Steve Garvey - Episode 24," Criteria For Success, January 3, 2020, https://criteriaforsuccess.com/lets-talk-sales-inspirational-quote-from-steve-garvey-episode-24/.

Melanie continues to grow spiritually as she continually learns to watch her thoughts every moment and gain insights every day about the nature of the True Self. She thinks it's the ultimate adventure.

But it's been a challenging path to follow. She struggled with her smoking, and it took her a long time to understand the road to the enlightenment she desired. She gradually learned the advantage of depending on herself for happiness and fulfillment instead of external sources.

She gave in to temptation several times on her journey but got back on track before it was too late because she was in good company. She was constantly reminded of her goal and inspired by others on the path.

So, you see, in Melanie's case, the Buddhist community helped her achieve the small goals that will hopefully lead to her big goal of enlightenment. One cannot set a deadline for enlightenment, but she realizes it is the purpose of her life, so she strives to stay motivated.

If you're a writer who wants to get published, you could join a writer's workshop. If you'd like to become a golf champion, join a golf club. An aspiring artist could live in an artists' community for inspiration and support.

All of us have the hero within us, waiting to be discovered. Effectively setting goals that matter leads you to become the best you can be and enjoy the happy life you deserve.

BIOGRAPHY

Kevin Goodnight is an ex-combat medic turned professional business consultant, coach, and author of several industry books. With over three decades of business consulting, Kevin has a unique perspective that shines through in his consulting systems. Kevin lives and works in Maryland, where he works with clients all over the world who are stuck and need that new perspective.

Connect with Kevin Goodnight via https://linktr.ee/kgoodnight

CHAPTER 2

Journey To Success

By Matt Morris

As a speaker and coach for the past twenty years, I've been blessed to help several thousand people become full-time entrepreneurs with hundreds in the six-figure range and over fifty documented million-dollar earners.

It's also rewarded me with a lifestyle that I never would have imagined as a boy. If you would have told me I'd be a millionaire at twenty-nine, earn eight figures in my thirties and generate several billion in sales, all while adventuring to over eighty countries by my early forties; I wouldn't have believed you.

I also never imagined I'd be blessed with a career that fills me up with such immense levels of fulfillment and significance, knowing that I've been able to assist so many others in achieving what most would consider "boundless" levels of success.

The question I'm asked all the time is . . . How?

In asking that question, most people are looking for tactics and strategies. And I'll admit, early in my coaching days, I focused my mentorship almost solely on teaching the how-tos.

Unfortunately, that made me a pretty lousy coach.

I'd give them the tactics that allowed me to become a superstar salesperson, run a multi-million dollar company, or speak powerfully from stage.

My students would apply the how-tos and come back frustrated with mediocre improvements at best.

What I failed to realize in my early coaching days is a quote from the late Brian Klemmer that says, "If how-tos were enough, we'd all be rich, skinny, and happy."

As we explore the secrets to experiencing boundless levels of success, we must first examine what keeps us bound to our current situation.

Hint: It's NOT a lack of tactics and strategies.

With a quick google search, you can find hundreds of YouTube videos and blog posts that will teach you the strategies to having six-pack abs. The reason most don't have that six-pack isn't that they don't know the how-tos.

When it comes to making your goals a reality, whether that be to have a sexy body, to become a top sales leader in your company, to start your own business, or any other worthwhile dream, the ONLY thing holding you back from achieving that goal is your mental programming.

The challenge most face in achieving a grand visionary future for themselves is the fact that it runs so completely contrary to their current vision, or identity, that's running them now.

Your current identity is made up of the beliefs you currently hold to be true about yourself. It's essentially how you genuinely see yourself.

Your personal identity subconsciously influences every decision and action you make (or don't make), thus influencing the level of success you're able to achieve.

If your personal identity is that of someone who is out of shape or overweight, you may go on streaks where you eat right and exercise vigorously, but you tend to always shift right back into your old ways.

Irresistible cravings, lethargy, sleeping in, etc., are somehow always overpowering your desire to be fit.

Why is that the case?

You'll want to write this down.

The Law of Commitment and Consistency

The law of commitment and consistency says that we will remain committed to remaining consistent with who we genuinely believe we are.

That being true, we must understand that in order to change our results, we have to change the beliefs we have about ourselves.

Let's take a deep dive into beliefs.

Take a look at the middle three letters of the word "beliefs," and what word do you see?

LIE

Consider for a moment that the story (the beliefs) you've been telling yourself about who you are as a person are simply lies you've made up.

Stories you may have accepted as "fact" like you're:

- Shy
- Self-conscious
- Lacking self-confidence
- Not a morning person
- Afraid of public speaking
- Not a good communicator
- Not as smart as the others

Would it be empowering to know that any of the negative beliefs above, along with countless others, are nothing more than lies you created subconsciously through a belief-building process you went through and didn't even know you were going through it?

What makes me so certain these "character traits" are lies? Because I had all of those beliefs about myself that I once accepted as fact.

Today, if you told me I was any of those things, I would laugh in your face because it would be completely absurd in my mind to accept any of those as true.

If you're willing to take a journey with me, I'll show you how I literally rewrote my entire identity from a broke, scarcity-filled, self-conscious young man into a confident and powerful multi- millionaire.

I'm here to tell you that whatever limiting beliefs you've created for yourself are absolute and total crap. I'm proof of it and many of those I've mentored for the past twenty years are proof of it.

I don't know what lies about yourself you've accepted as fact, but I know beyond a shadow of a doubt that, at your core, you are not a bad communicator, you are not unworthy of finding love, you are not a failure, you are not destined to always struggle, or any other negative belief.

Whatever they might be, you have the power to change those disempowering beliefs that serve only to limit the amount of success and personal fulfillment you experience.

If your current beliefs are what determine your success, the big question becomes how do you change your beliefs to create the results you want?

Before we answer that question, you first need to understand what shapes your beliefs in the first place. What has caused you to hold the beliefs that you do? Understanding where they came from will help you change them.

The belief building process you went through to come up with the beliefs you currently hold to be true have been shaped by three main factors:

1. Experiences
2. External programming
3. Internal programming

Experiences:

Every experience you've ever been through has been forever deposited and stored somewhere in your subconscious mind.

Maybe you were teased as a kid in school because you stuttered, and now you believe you're a poor communicator. Maybe you were laughed at in class as a kid for giving the wrong answer, and you took on a belief that you're not as smart as the other kids. Maybe you made a few horrible business choices when you were first starting out, and now you think you're lousy in business.

Whether you've realized it before now or not, those deposits were the first major factor that gave you the foundation of your identity.

Here's the way it works . . .

An event happens and then you make up a story (a belief) about what that event means.

Most of us tend to create a negative meaning based on what we perceive to be a negative experience. We create a victim story— I'm not loved because my parents abused me or left me. I'm a terrible business person because I failed for five years. People are not trustworthy because my business partner stole from me (all personal stories I made up at one point).

Think about some examples from your past. Can you think of some examples of events where you created a negative belief?

Real power comes from understanding that nothing has meaning until we give it meaning.

Events are neutral. It's the story we make up from the event that holds all the power. Rather than the victim story you may have been running in your mind, how can you create a new and empowering meaning based on that experience?

Understand—you have the power to choose. Victim or Victor. Which will it be?

External Programming:

Whether you want to believe this or not, you've been programmed. Your parents programmed you as a child to believe certain things about yourself, other people, money, religion, and many other things.

The school system, your friends, the media, television, and other factors have programmed you to believe many of the things you do today.

Some of this programming has likely been healthy and gotten you to where you are and built you into the person you are today. Unfortunately, we also all have some less than empowering beliefs, and associated fears, that we've adopted as well from that external programming.

By the time you were two years old, you heard the word no thousands of times more than you heard the word yes. It's no wonder so many people, when presented with an opportunity to start a business or take on a challenge, are paralyzed with fear and are hesitant to take action.

At some point in your life, you've most likely faced a moment where someone said something negative to you or doubted your ability, without even meaning to. For a lot of people, that first comes from their parents and family members.

The things that people say to you, whether they intentionally mean harm or not, can profoundly shape who you are—*but only if you let it.* You obviously can't go back into the past and change the negative things you've heard, but you can make the decision right now to no longer let those things define you.

You can recognize that what someone says about you has no basis in reality unless you *choose* to believe it. It's a choice. A choice you can start making right now, today, to say **no more**.

Internal Programming:

More than your experiences and more than the voices of the people around you, the greatest and most powerful way your beliefs are shaped is from your internal programming. Thankfully, it's also the mechanism you have the most control over.

Every word that comes out of your mouth and every thought that comes out of your mind serves as a programming tool. Those thoughts and words get entered into your subconscious mind and then work to create your habitual routines and mental thought patterns.

Psychologists who study brain science agree that your subconscious mind is infinitely more powerful than your conscious mind. The subconscious is the driving force behind your belief system and your identity.

The subconscious mind has a goal that can serve you negatively or positively. That goal is to keep you in line with your identity. Remember the law of commitment and consistency?

If, based on your regular programming, you tell yourself you're broke, you're tired, and you suck as an entrepreneur, your subconscious mind figures out a way to keep you consistent with that programming.

If, however, you continually tell yourself you're wealthy, you're energized, and you're an amazing entrepreneur, your subconscious mind begins doing everything in its power to create *that* reality.

Here's the best way to understand it.

Whatever you say about yourself makes it more true.

If you say, *"I'm an idiot,"* you become more of an idiot. If you say, *"I'm a genius,"* you become more of a genius.

Your consistent programming creates your identity.

Here's the trick; your subconscious mind does not know the difference between the truth and a lie. It simply does its best to carry out exactly what you've programmed it to believe.

So when you say, "I'm sexy, I'm confident, I'm a millionaire," your conscious mind might be telling you you're full of it, but your subconscious mind, which is where the true power lies, will take that as a command and start working out a way for you to be all of those things.

The key to reprogramming your subconscious and changing your deep-seeded beliefs is to change your deposits. You do this by constantly filling your subconscious mind with empowering, uplifting, and motivating thoughts and words.

If you continually profess what you don't want, or focus on the things you don't have or aren't, then you actually attract more of that negativity and continue to reinforce more of that personal identity. **What you focus on expands.**

BIOGRAPHY

Author of the international bestseller, *The Unemployed Millionaire*, Matt Morris began his career as a serial entrepreneur aged eighteen. Since then, he has generated over $1.5 billion through his sales organizations, with a total of over one million customers worldwide. As a self-made millionaire and one of the top internet and network marketing experts, he's been featured on international radio and television and spoken from platforms to audiences in over twenty-five countries around the world. And now, as the founder of Success Publishing, he co-authors with leading experts from every walk of life.

Contact Matt Morris via http://www.MattMorris.com

CHAPTER 3

The Person You Could Have Been

By Steve Moreland

If Fate's blood-stained cauldron has not found your life yet, she's hiding just over the horizon, waiting until you're at your most vulnerable. So if you're willing to listen to someone that knows about life's ash heap, I'll share the Lessons I learned *after* I failed my Test. The lessons focus on our thinking. More specifically, about how thinking differently empowered me to *thrive* where most cannot imagine surviving. I promise not to waste your time with fluffy bullshit or rah-rah! Just the mental tools what worked, that brought me across a desert wilderness of 5,544 days.

May the following battle-tested advice return you from your seemingly impossible cauldron *"tested—and found not wanting."*

We Texans pride ourselves on our Code. Toughness is Rule #1. And it means *"no tears allowed."* See, our cult-like indoctrination begins the moment we are born. And the other Spartan rules include: *do only BIG things*, especially if others say it can't be done; *rub some dirt on it* because blood and scars prove your worth; and *do Right*, even if the Lord God, himself, threatens you to do otherwise!

Brutal. Absolutely! But definitely the kind of folks you'd want covering your back in a fight. It's a belief carved deep in our soul—that there simply is NO FREE LUNCH. It is a creed rooted in commitment and perseverance, summed up in one word. Grit! The standard we have to carry begins early. At age twelve, I started *"earning my worth."* My phone rang off the wall with grass- cutting jobs in the Texas infernos called summer because my dad drilled me to do what everyone else is afraid of, to deliver results beyond expectations. Just self-disciplined results! No excuses.

I went right to corporate America after graduating with academic scholarships – working for three Fortune 500 companies before I was 24. At twenty-five I was in charge of my own brokerage firm in Dallas. By thirty, I'd made it to millionaire status, flew in private jets, brokered 9-figure deals from European castles, banked in numbered Swiss accounts, and spoke on international stages raising millions for venture capital deals.

Ballistic was my term for the vertical climb I experienced. Simultaneously serving as vice president of offshore operations for a boutique hedge fund, CEO of a 58-office tax and wealth management firm, and co-principal of a SaaS startup. I couldn't afford the luxury of sleep. And part of every month, I lived near my office in the banking district of Nassau, Bahamas, acting as the vice president of business development for a middle eastern banking syndicate.

Occasionally, I woke up at a place my then-wife and children called home. It was there that I slowed down enough to rub some of that Texas dirt on my hand tremors from sleeping only on those overseas flights. I was stumbling forward just to maintain the pace. There was something wrong but I could not risk failing the mission. My Dad's standing orders were crystal: *"You can rest when you're dead!"* And this belief came from his creed that a man only earns a medal on his gravestone if he dies "in combat."

Well, I failed to become a "lifer" in the Corps, so I determined that I was going to achieve whatever most would call impossible. I believed in his invincibility! And after eighteen years of his Marine-style bootcamp, I feared only one thing, **"meeting the person I could have been!"**

So, when Fate's blood-stained hurricane came for me, I was Ready. Ready to blindly march into Hell itself. But after the first few years, I felt more like the Greek myth of Sisyphus who was sentenced to pushing a boulder up the mountain every damn day and then waking up the next morning to find it at the bottom again. I remember thinking to myself, "Maybe God is *not* good" after feeling soul-crushing agony for the first time. Real pain that made me wish I could just die and get it over.

I'll admit, all that invincibility crap did NOT work. And I'm painfully embarrassed to admit that I found myself wallowing in my self-pity after losing absolutely everything and feeling abandonment by all I loved. I had succumbed to that state of a *victim*. And you know what, that Texas dirt did NOT fix the wounds I'd caused my family for the undeserved trials and tribulations my bull-headed foolishness caused.

Though I was brought up with my dad's relentless Texan and Marine Corp code of conduct mixed with my mom's Christian beliefs, the devasting pain caused me to question their beliefs. Sitting in the ash heap of my life like the Bible's character Job, I commenced to blaming God for not protecting us from the horror that imprisoned us. I begged and even prayed for an instant release of misery, even raising my fist in anger and shouting "You're *NOT* a good god!"

I just wanted that magical snap of a finger and everything to be like it used to be. But genie-like fixes never happen, do they. Why? Because strength is *not* forged in luxury and comfort. Medals do not get pinned to your chest for holding hands and singing "Kum Ba Yah."

The struggle to endure real agony, to eat suffering, and know your pain so intimately that you name her has a purpose. You see, it took time for me to get over my self-entitlement in order to face my demons and do the most excruciating thing I'd ever done. Realizing that I could not change the past or erase what my mistakes had cost my family, I had to make a decision: either continue to blame others and wallow in self-pity or use the hell I was inside to forge a better version of me!

In school, we're first taught the lesson that prepares us for the test. But, in life, we face the Test first; later, we learn the Lesson.

The grade is what we become through it all. It's pass or fail. And yes, hell is when you meet that person you could have been. It means rising again and again within the blood-stained cauldron of Fate. Only this repeated discipline distinguishes the few from the many, the extraordinary from the ordinary. The worthy from the worthless.

But that person you could have been is only Hell if he or she stands better than you chose to become! **Hell, then, is meeting the *better* person you could have been.**

Like I promised in the beginning, what follows WILL take you through any hell. And you will arrive on the other side, *"tested – and found not wanting."*

Let's begin with a question: "Have you ever been really curious about something—to the point of obsession?"

Since I was a kid, I wanted to unravel this thing called thinking. I reasoned to myself that if I could only understand how the few we call "great" actually thought, I might be able to be like them and make the world a little bit better. Because, for the most part, they are human just like me. The only difference is that they *see things differently* in their minds.

Personal development "coaches" blather about managing our thinking. It is THE key, agreed. But it's not enough to know *what* to do. We've got to know *how* to do it. It's the subtle and often <u>hidden difference between learning science without the art</u> <u>of knowing how it</u> <u>applies to real-world situations.</u> Most of these "well-meaning" coaches deserve an "A" for science but an "F" in art. Never earning a medal from within Fate's blood-stained cauldron means their theories can get you to one destination – that chance to meet the person you could have been.

Here's an example of a coach with earned rank, Dr. Viktor Frankl – author of *Man's Search For Meaning*. Frankl didn't just survive six years of Nazi concentration camps, he changed the world forever with his discovery of how we create meaning through our imagination.

Better thinking creates better doing. And better doing creates a better being.

Frankl forced me to think. I mean really think. And all of a sudden, what Professor Eli Goldratt wrote in *The Goal* became crystal clear. "If we continue to do what we have done, which is what everybody else is doing, we will continue to get the same *unsatisfactory* result." But I asked myself, isn't that what we do so very often - more of what everyone else has done and then expecting a different outcome?

We are what we've done, right? So, aren't our own actions - what we *do* - that creates who we *become*? In short, "doing creates being." So, who we are today – our being, is a product of our past doings? Becoming someone better can only happen by doing differently. And differently results from the seed of the thoughts in our imagination.

Because I wanted a different future – one that honored the sacred by making the world better, I could no longer afford to think like I used to, or like everyone else. Maybe you're brighter than me and already know this. But for me, this realization was the Eureka! And in that realization, I felt something deep inside like lightning.

If my prior thinking caused my current doings (my actions and habits that are known as my reality), **then why couldn't I change my future by changing the way I was thinking?**

Socrates (Greek philosopher 470 B.C.) taught a Secret passed through his student Plato to his student Aristotle (Greek philosopher 384 B.C.). Aristotle planted this Secret into the mind of a 13-year-old prince. This Secret method of thinking changed the ancient world.

At 16 years of age, the prince led his cavalry at the Battle of Chaeronea, decimating a supposedly unbeatable enemy. At 20 years of age, he became king of Greece, marched his army towards Persia, solved the riddle of the Gordian Knot, and destroyed any that opposed.

At 24, he captured the supposedly unconquerable city of Tyre. At 25, he became Pharaoh of Egypt and then returned to the desert near modern-day Babylon to lead his 50,000-man army against a force exceeding 500,000 led by the Persian emperor Darius. Charging into the front line on his legendary black stallion Bucephalus, he achieved the impossible and became emperor of the known world.

By age 30, he had created the largest empire in history. Today, he's still studied in war colleges for his battlefield genius, ethical governance, and unrivaled valor.

The Secret thought? "Be as you wish to seem."

The Result? One *impossible* difficulty after another - CRUSHED!

His Name? Alexander

How is he remembered? Alexander—the Great!

In school, we're first taught the lesson that prepares us for the test. But, in life, we face the Test first; later, we learn the Lesson.

Here's my experience. The Lessons learned *after* the Test lead to better actions—which lead to becoming a better being, right? That means that tests uncover our weaknesses so that we can learn greater lessons. What and who we become through the Tests reflects our grade in life.

If we're honest, we'll admit that we often create our own storms. And then we blame others when we must endure them. But if we use the agony, we find something called grit. Grit is commitment bathed in love to become better than we were the day before. It's a relentless dedication to rise—to become better, stronger, and wiser. It's a refusal to quit, even when we feel we can't get up again.

The question is, will we? Will we persist after the problems that were caused by our poor thinking – and the results that followed? Or will we just quit due to the fear of failing and the probability that life won't be easy?

Being *"tested and found not wanting"* means we'll certainly be scarred from one battle after another. But the scars reflect rank, defining how many times we returned to the cauldron instead of hiding and waiting to be rescued by the God that's testing us.

It may be cliché, but our very thinking sparks our every action. Put another way, our doings, added together over time, construct our being - *what* and *who* we become.

Do we dishonor the Sacred, settling for what everybody else is doing and continuing to get their same *unsatisfactory* results?

Or do we ***think* better**, in order to ***do* better**, so that we could ***be* better**?

We become what we choose to be. This is the Secret. My gift to you, as Aristotle long ago shared with Alexander, "be[come] as you wish to seem."

Now you know that Hell is NOT meeting the person you could have been.

Hell is meeting the *better* person you could have been.

BIOGRAPHY

A native Texan, Steve Moreland is known for two things. Dedicated practice. And success. Success equates to one's level of practice. So he really does only one thing. His Rubicon system teaches how to perform the common under uncommon conditions. Motivated by the Latin creed FORTES FORTUNA ADIUVAT – "Fortune favors the brave," his mission is to deliberately cause affirmative outcomes that would not have occurred otherwise.

Connect with Steve via https://linktr.ee/steve_moreland

CHAPTER 4

Being Enough

By Ann Riedy

Ever meet a person who everyone seems to love? The funny one, fun to be around, and a people magnet—always laughing or making others laugh. I always liked to be around a person like that because they made me feel like I was a part of something that I could never experience by myself.

I've always called myself shy. I was the shadow. I was someone who needed to be by someone's side and didn't like to be left to my own devices as I couldn't find anything to say. So, I became the shadow.

I can't say I liked it. I've always wanted to be like everybody else, and I wondered, 'What is wrong with me?' I never felt like I was enough. I didn't understand myself or why I was the way I was—living in the shadow but not enjoying myself along the journey. The struggle was real, and the harsh judgment towards self was constant.

One day, I heard someone say that you become what you think about all day long. I wondered what the heck that meant because my thoughts were not too kind to me. I started the process of really analyzing what and why my thoughts kept me busy all day long, and I wanted to find out what I could do to change it.

One day I realized something important: "I am Enough!"

"I am Enough!" Have you ever said that yourself? I hope you have, and I hope you do every single day because it is the truth.

YOU ARE ENOUGH! YOU ARE AWESOME! YOU ARE BEAUTIFUL! YOU ARE AMAZING! YOU ARE SO BRAVE!

Although, chances are that if you are like me, you haven't said those words. But if you said those words as a small child, you might have been made to feel like it was wrong or that you were being conceited and full of yourself. After all, that is not something we wanted to be.

Last year, I had some time on my hands during the pandemic, and I joined a couple of coaching classes. One of the sessions opened my eyes to a whole lot of stuff, one of which is this lie we tell ourselves: we are *not* enough.

It sounds something like this:

I don't know enough. I don't look good enough. My voice isn't good enough. I'm not tall, thin, cute, young, clever, or whatever enough. I'm just not good enough. I didn't say enough. I didn't do enough. I should have . . . I shouldn't have . . .

You get the drift.

I learned about something called our inner critic and how it always looks for something to keep us down, stop us from moving forward, and hold us still. One of the classes talked about something that really spoke to me: *The Vow to Be Invisible*. Wow! That spoke to me because it was how I felt about putting myself out there in the world to offer my help to people because of all the reasons stated above: the whole 'I'm not enough' saga and the inner critic taking over and keeping me silent.

Once I had a name for all this "stuff" going on in my head, I could finally take action because, before that, I had no idea what made me so different. I hadn't the slightest clue of what made me stay silent and not move forward to achieve my greatness, goals, and my own unique ability to connect with people.

One time, a coach from one of the classes I attended asked me a few questions about my goals and passions in life. I had a hard time answering her. But I *did* know that if others could do it, so could I.

You see, I love to learn, study, and share the information I'm learning with anyone who needs it. And when I revealed to someone all the books I'd read and all the "binders" of notes from classes I'd taken, I was told,

"Ann, you know enough!"

"You know enough to fill many lifetimes of helping people!"

"You just need to 'feel' like you *are* enough, and everything will change in your life."

Really??? Well, how do you go about all of this?

I'm going to share with you the three most important steps that I took to help me overcome these inner critical voices and step into my greatness. I will show you how you can confidently, and without reserve, say to yourself boldly, "I AM ENOUGH! I AM AWESOME! I AM BEAUTIFUL, I AM AMAZING, and I AM SO BRAVE!"

I'm sure you've heard the saying, 'You become what you think about all day long' or 'You become what you say to yourself.' Other variations include 'what you are listening to' and 'what you hear every day.'

If the above is true, we really need to examine what that means, and more importantly, what it is that we hear every day that affects our lives and makes us who we are.

So, let's dive into the three steps you can take to begin the process of leaning into the true, wonderful feeling of *I Am Enough*!

Step One

The first part of the first step is to be aware of and examine your self-talk. Are you kind or critical of yourself? More importantly, what desires and beliefs lie deep inside of you? Who is your private self, your invisible self, that you don't let anyone see? You know that quiet little space inside of you that no one can get to, that no one can ruin. It's a secret. Do you see that person inside of you?

The second part of this step is to uncover and write down some of those thoughts and feelings. Write down your secret thoughts of who you *know* you really are or who you wish you were to the world. Also, write down the names of anyone you admire and why you admire them.

Step Two

Make a list of positive statements about being enough. No critical, negative statements. Only loving, kind, and compassionate words.

Some examples of these statements are:

I am enough.
I am beautiful enough.
I am full, thin, or fit enough.
I love enough.
I am strong enough.
I am smart enough.
I am whole and complete at this moment.
I am perfect just as I am.
I love big.
I am totally enough in the package, with all these flaws (*name the flaws*).
I am significant.
I have a gift.
I matter.
I am lovable.
I am here for a reason.

Whether you believe in the good or bad, you are always going to be right. You can fool the brain to believe whatever you tell it, and it will manifest whatever it is. So, why not use positive words instead of negative?

I read a sentence someone once wrote: "Don't speak about what is. Speak about what you want things to be, and what you think and speak will come to you."

Your mind does not care what you tell it—good, bad, healthy, or unhealthy. It will start to give you more of whatever is in it. Always make it good and healthy.

Write it all down and repeat it out loud to yourself several times a day.

At first, it will feel like you are lying to yourself. It's okay. Who you really and truly are is good and perfect, loving and kind, and enough, just as you are. You do not have to change. You just need to accept the flaws that come along with the picture of the good you have drawn for yourself.

So, go ahead and start telling yourself amazing things about your amazing self. You will begin to feel these things become a reality.

I remember when I first did this. I called it my "sleep tape." I would say my positive statements while on my treadmill, and I didn't believe most of them. But I kept at it over and over. I felt silly. I felt like a fraud and that it was all a lie. Then, at night, I would put my headphones on and listen as I slept.

Well, today, when I look at those statements, I actually believe them to be true, even though I genuinely thought they were lies and that I didn't deserve them at another time in my life.

It will happen to you too. Just trust the process and *take action*!

Step Three

Practice your own form of meditation, or what I like to call "quiet silence," preferably in a place where you can be quiet. Do something intentionally, like going for a long walk, sitting and drinking that favorite hot drink, guided meditation maybe, or engrossed in reading a book. It can be anything that quiets your mind and helps you be aware of a world bigger than you.

When you become intentional about doing those things every day to get into that quiet space, all kinds of fantastic things start to happen. Awareness begins to take over things that can change your life today and tomorrow. What do I mean by that? Well, people, ideas, and things come into our life, and we will be able to "see" them. We will be aware of them like magic, and we start to expect things to pop up—things that appear through magic, fate, or an unknown force that we don't quite understand.

We need to spend time in this quiet space so we can tap into unknown aspects of life—the awareness of what we can't really explain with words.

You must start somewhere—even with five minutes a day. As you move forward with your days, awareness of a thought or a beautiful scene or the smell of an amazing flower will fill your being, and you will experience the profound wonder of what is to be *for me*. What am *I* here for? What is *my* purpose?

You will get out of the 'I am not enough' space into those of 'I want to be more,' 'I want to be enough,' 'I want to learn what it's all about,' and 'I want it now!'

The journey has been ongoing for me, but it is an exciting adventure. I'm beginning to realize that the "hard" and "dark" times in life are when I can learn the most and begin to fly in the right direction, and trust in the process of life, growth, and love.

So, I wish for you this day to find that quiet space and just listen. The still quiet voice inside of you will sound through just a whisper of a thought. Notice it, and take action.

You will never be sorry you took those moments for yourself. I hope you find yourself living the truth of who you are and be able to say with belief, "I AM ENOUGH!"

BIOGRAPHY

Ann Riedy is a retired registered nurse who set aside her career and dedicated her energies to entrepreneurship. This allowed her to become a business owner in her early thirties. She feels the most important aspect of success is ongoing personal growth and development. Ann started creating her own stories and expressing the world through her eyes when she was very young. She started writing blog posts and sharing her stories on her social media sites. Her unique and engaging writing style taps into the minds and hearts of all who read her work. Ann lives and works out of her home in Eastern Montana. She spends her free time enjoying walks along the river and going on adventures with her grandchildren.

Connect with Ann Riedy via https://linktr.ee/annriedy

CHAPTER 5

Roller Coaster Ride

By Blanca E. Rodriguez

Have you ever thought about how much of a roller coaster ride life can be? The ups, downs, turn arounds, loops, stops, and go's. Anthony Bourdain said, "Your body is not a temple, it's an amusement park. Enjoy the ride."[2]

I was born into mental illness on both my mother's and father's sides of the family. Many aunts, uncles, cousins, and even siblings had or have some kind of mental disability: everything from psychosis, PTSD, schizophrenia, obsessive-compulsive disorder, severe anxiety, bipolar disorder, and more. So does my mother. She grew up with extreme poverty, malnourishment, neglect, and abuse. She still went to school, got a job, and made her way through life the best way she could. I'm very proud of her for that.

My mother suffers from chronic depression and dementia. Of course, she wasn't properly diagnosed until her late seventies. Most of us were raised in a culture where mental illness would be the equivalent

---

2 "A Quote from Kitchen Confidential," Goodreads (Goodreads), accessed November 2, 2021, https://www.goodreads.com/quotes/271353-your-body-is-not-a-temple-it-s-an-amusement-park.

of a 'Your-life-is-over' kind of thing. We thought that the "crazy" people were only the ones that went to the psychiatric ward.

Like my mother, my father was raised in a large family with limited resources. Some siblings had mental illnesses. Still, he made it to college, joined the military, traveled the world, and was even a math teacher. But his biggest dream was to become an entrepreneur. He married my mom and moved from Puerto Rico to New York City to fulfill his dream. My father, uncle, and some of their friends moved to Brooklyn in the late 1950s, searching for a better life.

They went through many hardships to fulfill their goals and make the American Dream a reality. With very hard work and dedication, Papa opened a jewelry store and owned the apartment building where we used to live. My father made his dream come true; he was an entrepreneur. It was between the mid-1960s and early 1970s.

Life was beautiful until that fateful day of November 10, 1973. An armed robbery gone terribly wrong led to my father's death; life was never the same again.

According to many psychologists, our beliefs start when we are children—the time when fear, trauma, and self-identity begin to take hold.

I was eight years old when my father died. We were growing up in an environment where you didn't "talk about the dead." Being the youngest of three siblings, my family called me 'stupid' a lot, and just because I was a little kid, my words had no credibility. I remember family members telling me, 'You talk when the chickens pee.' Of course, this only increased my trauma and low self-esteem. I assumed that it was wrong to talk about anything; no one heard my voice anyway.

Don Miguel Ruiz says in his book *The Four Agreements*, "Don't make assumptions."[3] I committed many mistakes in my life because of

3   "The Four Agreements Quotes by Miguel Ruiz," Goodreads (Goodreads), accessed November 2, 2021, https://www.goodreads.com/work/quotes/376130-the-four-agreements-a-practical-guide-to-personal-freedom-a-toltec-wis.

assuming rather than reaching out to someone and speaking out.

When I was nine years old, I was sexually assaulted for the first time. I was coming home from school, passing by a walkway between houses, and there he was, the street junkie I was so scared of. He was intimidating, looked mean, and he *was* mean. That day, he grabbed me. I never said anything about it. I was assaulted again by a cousin when I was twelve years old. It happened at home, the place where I was supposed to be safe. I assumed nobody would believe me and that it was somehow my fault. I was sexually assaulted and harassed for years to come.

Sexual harassment was a constant at any workplace, from the office building to the hotel industry, and most recently, as a massage therapist. I would report some of them, and they never heard my voice until my last boss believed my story, banned both patients (yes, patients) who harassed me, and helped with my recovery. For that, I am eternally grateful.

This kind of trauma brought me issues of low self-esteem, low self-worth, and no self-love. I was very promiscuous in my twenties; I didn't respect myself or my body. I never dealt with it or asked for the help I so very much needed and deserved. I drowned my insecurities and trauma with drugs, alcohol, and poor choices. Still, I managed to go to school, graduate with an associate degree, and have a promising dancing career.

Anthony Robbins says, "Where focus goes, energy flows."[4]

I was so focused on working for my weekends that my dancing career didn't prosper. I stopped dancing for many years. I tried to ignore the trauma for so long. My method of coping was denial, and at my lowest point, I became a "functional junkie." I always looked for

---

4   Team Tony, "Energy Flows Where Attention GOES - Focus & Energy: Tony Robbins," Tony Robbins, August 21, 2019, https://www.tonyrobbins.com/career-business/where-focus-goes-energy-flows/.

the next party, the next overindulgence, and the next guy to give me temporary satisfaction. I never took the time to rest, be alone, and take a long look at the mirror and ask, 'Where the hell is your life going?' Wow, the energy really did flow.

My relationship with my mother was close to nothing, and I hardly saw my siblings. I was at war with my mother; she had awful manic symptoms that only increased with time. She was too obsessed with all the siblings, too controlling, too verbally abusive, and cruel. I just didn't understand where this excessive anger was coming from. Mom could be the most loving person one minute and the most hateful the next. Her symptoms were only getting worse, and all of us siblings moved out of the house. It was unbearable to live in such a toxic environment. I totally disconnected myself from the situation; I ran away from it. I isolated myself in a world of denial, thinking that I would have it all figured out once I didn't live with my mother anymore.

I married my first husband out of impulse. We dated for a few months, and I got pregnant. I thought it was a chance to settle and have a family. Two days before the wedding, I suffered a miscarriage; I was devastated. I wanted to cancel the wedding, but I wasn't brave enough to do so. I was never in love with him. I assumed it would work out. We were married for three years. I was looking for the stability and love that I could only find within myself. It took me another fourteen years to finally realize that.

I started my relationship with my ex-partner (RIP) and father of my two kids as a casual, no-strings-attached relationship: going to the club, doing drugs, having sex, and bye, see you next time. As time passed, I got more obsessed with him. I wanted a serious relationship because I thought I was in love. We were never on the same page. I always knew he had drug issues. I assumed he would do better if I refused to do drugs. How wrong I was.

He had a chronic drug and depression problem that he never addressed. Nobody could save him but himself.

When I got pregnant, I immediately quit drugs and alcohol because I wanted to have a healthy baby. I was thirty-two years old. God gave me the miracle of a healthy boy! My very toxic relationship went on and off. Yet, I kept assuming that things would get better with breakups, distance, and the whole let's-get-back-together sort of thing. Three years later, I gave birth to a beautiful and healthy baby girl! Ever since I became a mother, my life only started to change drastically. I assumed that my partner would quit drugs, seek help, and be the incredible father I hoped he would be. News flash: my assumptions were all wrong. I made up that movie in my head.

Our relationship only got worse: a codependent, abusive, addictive, destructive, and horrible vicious circle. My trauma was still there, waiting for me to face it. Then one day, I started reading a book called *The Secret*. It was the beginning of my evolution and change. It was time to save myself.

Earl Nightingale says, "We become what we think about."[5]

From that moment on, I started to read any self-help book I put my hands on—anything from Carl Jung, Sigmund Freud, Anthony Robbins, Marianne Williamson, Bob Proctor, and Louise Hay. I secretly started to attend counseling. I began to have more faith in my capabilities, went to massage therapy school, and got certified as a group fitness and Zumba instructor. I was working at the best spas and medical offices in town and discovered holistic living.

My so-called love for my partner started to fade. I made a list of what I wanted in a gentleman. My life was shifting into something far away from the environment where my children and I were living. So, in

---

5   "We Become What We Think About," Transcend Your Limits, accessed November 2, 2021, https://www.transcendyourlimits.com/we-become-what-we-think-about/.

December 2011, three months after losing my beloved uncle and second father to his horrific and tragic death and me ending up being sick and having emergency surgery in the hospital, I left my ex-partner. I was alone with two little kids, a crappy car, and $89 in my bank account.

I received so much support from so many guardian angels. I went to live at a friend's house. Somehow my Aqua Zumba students found out what was happening, and they helped me with money. I received over $1,000 in cash and gift cards from all of these people! I'm forever grateful to them. It was the biggest blessing and the best decision I ever made at that point.

Napoleon Hill said in his book, *Think and Grow Rich*, "Faith removes limitation."[6]

The moment I started to believe in my strength and capabilities, things just kept on shifting and changing. I refused to keep raising my kids in an addictive, abusive, loveless, and codependent environment. We deserved so much better, and with faith, resilience, and focus, it worked out. I found the man of my dreams—the one I asked for on my list. He's my husband and my best friend. You see, freedom of the mind is truly possible.

In 2013, my ex-partner passed away. He was forty-eight years old. We did forgive each other. I learned a valuable lesson from him: Don't stay lost in the past. Seek help and speak up.

My relationship with my mother is wonderful. She got the help that she so very much deserved and needed. We have forgiven each other. I have a beautiful bond with my beloved sister. She is the godmother of both my kids. She is my best friend, my rock, and my hero.

I admit that my relationship with my brother could be better. We have a long-distance bond, even though we live in the same state. I truly

---

6   "Quote by Napoleon Hill, Think and Grow Rich," Quoteslyfe, accessed November 2, 2021, https://www.quoteslyfe.com/quote/Riches-begin-in-the-form-of-thought-138388.

believe every relationship is a two-way street, not a one-way road. I love my brother and will always be there for him no matter what.

My kids are grown adults now. They are amazing people. I apologized to them for all those dark years we endured as I was part of the problem.

Jim Rohn used to say, "Learn to work harder on yourself than you do on your job."[7] The moment I realized that my life's main goal was to heal my broken soul from trauma, neglect, sexual assault and harassment, low self-worth, and low self-esteem and that the only way to have a successful life is to love myself, that was when I started to blossom into the woman I am today.

I believe love and forgiveness are truly the heart of the matter.

Earl Nightingale said, "People with goals succeed because they know where they're going."[8]

I can tell you this: Don't let your past define your future. And now, more than ever, I definitely know where I'm going.

---

7   "A Quote by Jim Rohn," Goodreads (Goodreads), accessed November 2, 2021, https://www.goodreads.com/quotes/7898460-learn-to-work-harder-on-yourself-than-you-do-on.

8   "Earl Nightingale Quotes," BrainyQuote (Xplore), accessed November 2, 2021, https://www.brainyquote.com/quotes/earl_nightingale_383343.

BIOGRAPHY

Blanca E. Rodriguez has been a licensed massage therapist for sixteen years, a certified fitness instructor for over thirty years, and a certified canine massage therapist for seven years. She is also an entrepreneur, and now, an author! Her scope of practice is healthy senior living. She's a member of the Pan American Round Table of the Treasure Coast (an organization that provides scholarships for students in need) and a member of the Holistic Education Foundation, focusing on helping the community experience wellness with a more holistic approach. She is an animal lover, and her mission is to help others feel better and succeed. Her goal is to touch 500,000 lives with her story of resilience, hope, and never giving up. She lives in Florida with her husband of eight years and their dog. They share four kids, all adults now.

Connect with Blanca E. Rodriguez via https://linktr.ee/r.blancae

CHAPTER 6

A Word To Influencers

(A Prelude to My Upcoming Book "Success Secrets of Moguls: The Power Behind the Success")

By Evangelist Cheryl Green

Statistics say that nearly 100 million sperm compete for one egg. But only one sperm fertilizes the egg. Then, the fertilized egg must continue in the womb and keep developing. Chances for non-development are enormous. But God says, "I want *you* to exist…You are *chosen*." God has a divine purpose for every person He creates.

I had a direction I wanted to go, a purpose I wanted to pursue. And God changed it.

You do not choose destiny. Destiny chooses you.

I had dreams, hopes, and aspirations; I had places that I wanted to go, places that excited and enthused me.

But God came into my life, wrecked my plans, wrecked my dreams, and took away my stuff. He interrupted my life. And then, He led me to something else.

My life has been like a play, where they close the curtain and then open it to a completely different scene. Sometimes, it's dark, and I can't see what's before me. But that's only because God has temporarily closed the curtains, so He can set up the props and put stuff in place for the next phase of my life. Then, He opens the curtains. And the scene is totally different from what I expected. The scene feels like an interruption, like I am all turned around. But God has the last say.

I had a specific plan for my life, and my child interrupted that plan.

God has taught me that He did not make a mistake giving me Irene. He created her and sent her to me exactly as He desired, giving her a distinct personality. She was given to me, not merely to raise but also for God to use her to grow me into the person He has created me to be. It is not God's intention to destroy us through the test. It is His intention to make us, mold us, and show us that He can sustain us in the midst of it all. God used Irene to reveal to me fresh insights about His character and mine. I count it as an honor that He thought me special enough to raise this special child with special needs. God specializes in special assignments. And now, God has given me my latest special assignment...

This is it. You have entered the mist of the rhapsodist, a spiritual, a miracle, an evangelist: a prophetic, poetic daughter of the King, enlarging the territory of the hip-hop scene. God has given me a revelation that He will use rap as a unique way of addressing the entire nation. Hip-hop is a powerful tool. It has reached so far across the world. Righteous rap, God's radical combination of Jesus, spirituality, and hip-hop are a channel to reach out to the discouraged and the lost. Rappers may seem like the least likely candidates for God to use, but music is a universal language. Rap and hip-hop are the most popular styles of music in the world today. God is issuing a clarion call for us to recognize that the power of rap can be harnessed to spread the Word of God and that many of today's biggest emcees are the perfect shepherds for the cause. They are divorced from every allegiance but the Almighty. They have no desire to fit into churchology or impress others. God's next generation of leaders will not be tied to church systems, religious systems, people, departments, denominations, auxiliaries, departments, circumstances, and organizations. When God says, "Move," they will not have to ask others.

God has gifted all of us the ministry of reconciliation, but today, there is a remnant of rappers and influencers to whom God has given special qualities of charisma. They have unique gifts of influence and charm and the power to inspire and persuade. And their gifts were given to them to glorify God and edify the body. When God breathes on these influencers, their souls are ignited. As Job said, "[T]he breath of the Almighty hath given me life" (Job 33:4 KJV). They will stand up and take dominion and authority over circumstances. God will call them to bring order to disorder and send a fatal blow to chaos and confusion, all for His glory. All our talents and gifts were given to us from God, to be used for Him. Gifts belong to God and are entrusted to us for our use. We may misuse a gift, but this does not take away from God's ownership. The ability and talent to rap or influence is a gift from God. The stewardship of a gift is one's gift to God.

Some people are under the assumption that rap is not "of God." Oh yes, it is! "In the beginning was the Word, and the Word was with God, and the Word was God. All things were made by Him; and without Him was not anything made that was made. In Him was life; and the life was the light of men. And the light shineth in darkness; and the darkness comprehended it not. And the Word was made flesh..." (Jn 1:1, 3-5, 14 KJV). The abstract was made concrete. The invisible was made visible. The intangible was made touchable. Our God is linguistic, speaking, and a language specialist. He is beyond intelligence, brilliance, encyclopedias, and computers. He is a *communicator*.

When God made humans, He created us to be communicators. No other species on the planet can communicate as fluidly or effectively as human beings. We were created in the image and likeness of a linguistic God. It is part of our Godlikeness to be able to communicate. And the more we become like God, the more effective we become at communicating. We are designed to be creative *communicators*. So, you see, rappers are MCs (master communicators) and rhapsodists.

The definition of rhapsody is an effusive, unrestrained, heart-felt, undignified praise to God. God will use rhapsody to bring billions to know His Son.

The battle today is for the minds of people. If you influence a person's beliefs, you influence the person as a whole. The only way we will change is by changing the way we think. We must reprogram ourselves with the right thinking. Our mind is very much like a computer. Sure, we can go out and buy the most expensive and powerful computer with the largest memory and the latest gadgets. But if we program that computer with the wrong software, it won't function properly. The problem is not the hardware; the problem is the operating system.

The same is true with us. You and I were fashioned in the image of the Almighty God. He is our manufacturer. When He created us, He made us to be victorious. From the beginning, He programmed us for success, joy, peace, and victory. God gave us good hardware. But we often allow the enemy to infiltrate our mind and soul and reprogram our software. However, God strategically takes every abuse, misuse, disaster, adversity, and weakness of ours to bring about a uniting effect.

Rappers who operate from their God-given callings will defy the order of the day—that status quo of today's rap music—with the radical infusion of Jesus into hip-hop. Music is a universal language. This "righteous rap" will reach Generation Next, impacting a group of people who may never otherwise enter a church building. It will seek and save the lost, edify believers, and restore families by bridging generational gaps. Righteous rap will revolutionize traditional forms of outreach.

As a genre, rap music dominates the entire world. Hip-hop is at the forefront of pop culture. It governs what is cutting edge in fashion trends and style. Hip-hop is a multi-billion-dollar industry. Even mainstream America is captivated by it, with its reach extending beyond borders, from Europe to Asia and even Down Under.

Hip-hop culture spans all ethnicities. It does not see color. At rap concerts, you see whites, blacks, browns, yellows, reds, and every color in between. This culture, this movement, has done a better job than the government and all the churches combined with bringing people of different nationalities together. Martin Luther King, Jr. said, "I think it is one of the tragedies of our nation, one of the shameful tragedies of our nation, that 11 o'clock on a Sunday morning is one of the most segregated hours, if not the most segregated hours, in Christian America."[9] This is because every race and ethnic group goes to their own churches.

Corruption is at an all-time high. Getting killed by police is a leading cause of death for young Black men in America. There are great social and economic disparities and inequalities among people of color. There are broken marriages and broken dreams. But despite all of this, I am encouraged. Righteous rap will go beyond recycling saints to rescuing and reclaiming a mass secular market, stimulating repentance and salvation, and impacting the world with healing and deliverance.

The message of salvation should cross all racial, social, and cultural barriers. We must develop strategies to reach every segment of the population. Righteous rap takes this message of salvation to all people and makes it accessible. When influencers and prominent rap artists stand before God, He will not ask them how many "streams" or "downloads" they got on their music or how many "views" or "likes" they had on their videos. Instead, He will ask them if they fulfilled

---

9   Sandhya Dirks, "Integrating Sunday Morning Church Service - A Prayer Answered," NPR (NPR, August 11, 2018), https://www.npr. org/2018/08/11/637552132/integrating-sunday-morning-church-service-a-prayer-answered.

their calling. Did they take advantage of their God-given notoriety and power of influence?

Jesus reached the lost with the Gospel and instilled Himself in men. But the work remains unfinished. **There are three desires that God has for influencers** (and each of us):

1. *God desires all of us to come to a saving knowledge of Jesus Christ. He desires that all men repent and be reconciled to Him. He sent His Son so that man might believe and receive eternal life* (Jn 3:16, Acts 17:30 and 2 Cor 5:20).

2. *God desires that we become spiritually mature and followers and imitators of Jesus Christ. We are not meant to remain spiritually immature children* (Rom 8:6).

3. *God desires that we become spiritual followers, imitators, and reproducers of Jesus Christ. We are to equip others so they can be sent out to reproduce Jesus Christ in others, in a third spiritual generation. This is the divine strategy for the continuation of the work of Christ* (Mk 11:15).

Christianity is about sharing this Gospel with those who have not heard it or who have lost their way. We must move from invitation to invasion. Ministry happens out in the world. We must speak the world's language. We must connect. In the Bible, you see that Jesus went everywhere. He was a friend to sinners. He accepted every person as they were. People felt comfortable around him.

There are two billion Christians on the planet, but there are seven billion inhabitants. The Lord uses every avenue available to spread the Gospel of influence. We are now in the midst of the most savage storm the world has ever known. Our society is riddled with greed, government corruption, terrorism, and war. Billions of people are bound with the chains of sin, sickness, poverty, and disease.

But there is an answer! Righteous rap is a channel to reach the lost. These influencers may seem like the least likely candidates for God to use. But as they operate from their God-given calling, they will buck convention and embrace rap as a modern form of rhapsody.

Great ministry is birthed out of great pain and shame. God does not waste anything. Although not all hip-hop is good, a good chunk of it does "work together for good" (Rom 8:28 KJV).

When The Lord gets ready to use someone, He does not choose religious people. He finds people who have been in the fire. Fire is what purifies you; it burns the mess out of you, teaches you, and it gives you a message to deliver. This message offers grace, mercy, forgiveness, and redemption. It is liberation, not incarceration. This is **God's Strategy for Influencers!**

BIOGRAPHY

Detroit, Michigan, is famous for owning the coveted title, "The Motor City" and breeding the hitmaker, "Motown Records." But now, this metropolis can add to its list of success stories, native Evangelist Cheryl Green, aka C-Money the Discipler—Minister-In-Rap! C-Money is a spiritual activist, anointed and appointed to glorify God, edify believers, and evangelize the world with the flow-style flavor of hip-hop righteous rap. Evangelist Cheryl Green is preparing to extend her ministry to audiences worldwide with the release of her debut book and record. Not ashamed to preach the Gospel, this prophetic and poetic rhapsodist professes she will proclaim God's unadulterated Word through this radical ministry to the unchurched and a society of youth who may never enter a church building!

Connect with Evangelist Cheryl Green
via https://linktr.ee/CherylGreenRhaps

CHAPTER 7

Expect The Unexpected

By Claudia Pugl

I woke up in a roof space, lying on a mattress on the concrete floor. The dusty environment came with a washing machine and a dryer next to it used by the residents of the house. There was no door and no privacy. It was basically a roof space used as a storeroom to do laundry. I asked myself: "How did I end up like this? How did I let it get this far?

My boyfriend (at the time) and I got kicked out of my apartment because of several arguments between him and my landlord. My ex-boyfriend was very quick-tempered, stubborn, and of course, his opinion was always the right one. We were living in the Netherlands at that time. He was originally from England and moved to the Netherlands because of his ex-girlfriend, a Dutch woman. I am originally from Germany and wanted to work abroad to broaden my horizon, learn a different language, meet new people, and enjoy other cultures. So, I ended up in the Netherlands after sending my CV to various countries like Norway, Sweden, and other European countries. I immediately got a job offer in the Netherlands. I'm a trained painter in construction, and I wanted to take up the challenge of working in another country and experience life on my own. Being a woman, it was a bit challenging to get a job as a painter at that time (2011). Women weren't that commonly found in that line of work—at least in Germany. It was a pleasant experience to see many more women working in this trade in the Netherlands when I started there. For them, it was totally normal and nothing special.

To be honest, I didn't know much about our neighbouring country other than the stereotypes of them making good cheese, having the typical Dutch wooden shoes called clogs, being popular for cycling a lot, and having plenty of weed. I know that's not a lot of knowledge to take there, but I was excited and curious to know more about the country, its people, and our differences and similarities. The more I got to know the country and the people, the more I liked it—so much so that I ended up spending almost six years there.

When I met my boyfriend, I thought I had found my soulmate and that we'd surely end up getting married, having kids, and building our own family. I thought I found the one, and that'd be it.

He had worked as a CNC machinist, but he was unfortunately fired after about half a year and didn't work for the next four years. He didn't have any sort of income, salary, or benefits. It became more and more difficult for me to pay for everything alone. Plus, there were his car projects—which, of course, were very important to him—and he wanted to get things finished. So, I was paying for all that as well. And if you know something about cars, they can get pretty expensive. When you love someone, you just try to help as much as possible, but you are also a bit blinded. In my case, I was giving up on myself. I was there for him, trying to help him because he was dissatisfied with not having work and being unable to finance his car projects. I started to lose myself and wasn't watching over myself. That's one thing I realised later: I made the mistake of putting him in the centre of attention in my life and not taking care of myself. It was as if I had blinders on and couldn't see reality.

Then, I lost my job because of the lack of orders. The company had to fire me, and I couldn't get another job because it was wintertime (during winter, there is way less work for painters), and there were no upcoming job prospects.

One bad thing led to another, and we began struggling with late payments. Then, the argument between my ex and landlord got us kicked out of the apartment. Luckily, he had friends who let us live in their roof space. Technically, it was a storeroom and not really a living space, but it was better than nothing at all—especially during the winter. Of course, it was for momentary survival. My ex had no income, no benefits, and no health insurance, and we had to pay for treatments when needed. I was jobless and did not want to admit to my family or friends that we were struggling because they already said he wasn't good for me. I wasn't ready to admit any of that.

So, we survived with things like collecting bottles and using the deposit for food. We'd also get the occasional side job, like painting a room or doing a car repair. Once a week, a friend of ours would invite us over for a hot meal. Of course, we didn't mention anything about our situation, but we were happy to have that nice, home-cooked meal once a week. Plus, they were Italian, and their cooking skills were just amazing.

We saved up some money we earned through the side jobs and decided to move to Germany, closer to my family. I quickly found work at a company in Austria that built airplane parts. It wasn't the perfect job—working in shifts—but it did provide an income. However, my ex could neither find a job nor hold onto one. Then, something unexpected happened one day: he met a woman online. At the time, it was unexpected. He broke up with me, left me with all our worries and debts, moved back to England, and is now married to her.

I was devastated. I had put so much time, money, and effort into the relationship. I had given up so much for his sake. I thought that going through the rough times we experienced would have deepened the bond between us. What I had invested was all gone. I lost all that time and effort. I am not talking about the money as much as all the love I had given. The dreams of 'back then' disappeared just like that. But what I failed to realize was that things hadn't been alright for a while. I didn't take care of myself and lost track. I didn't even know my own boundaries, and when you don't know your own, how can anyone else know them and treat you right? I had gained a lot of weight, and we were both unhappy and dissatisfied with our lives. When I look back, he did me a favour by breaking up with me.

So, now it was time to take care of myself and take responsibility for my health and well-being. I was a shy girl who didn't have enough confidence. I also carried a lot of self-doubts. I was always hiding because I put other people on a pedestal and considered myself small and unimportant. I always thought other people were more intelligent than me or more beautiful. I cared too much about what other people would think of me. I was always more of a listener and less of a talker. If you'd ask people about me, they would tell you that I was the one in the room who only listened but wouldn't talk. It was as if my brain was empty. Because I was so insecure, I didn't bring out the right words. I was physically there, but getting to know me would take a very long time because I didn't dare to open up. Something always held me back: it was me. I was too insecure, and I was in my own way. And for those people who didn't want to take that time to get to know me, we never got close. I was always an introvert and observed. What do I have to say? What do I know? I planted negative seeds in my brain for years and believed and acted that way. I never thought that I could be successful or that people would like me. I always assumed that other people had something against me.

Going back to my past, I grew up with my grandma and grandpa because my parents got divorced when I was six years old, and my dad had to travel a lot because of his work. My mum had depression and had to visit the clinic a couple of times. So, my grandparents raised me, and I am very thankful for that. When I look back at those times with my grandparents, it was a great time. I am grateful to have had such great grandparents, and they did a fantastic job raising me.

But ever since I was a kid, I always had that feeling of not being good enough. Later, I realised that I was the one who was planting the negative seeds in my brain. Never let negative experiences determine your future.

Now, after the breakup, being alone again, and having a lot of time to think and reassess everything, I came to the conclusion that I wanted to do something with my life. I decided to use the rest of my time wisely and do something meaningful. I started playing sports regularly and lost 20 kgs. I also did personal development. I worked on myself a lot, and I am now building my online business in the network marketing industry—something I would have deemed impossible in the past. I am even doing lives on social media and being present. I would have never started a conversation like that before. I am getting out of my comfort zone and doing things I would have previously never done. I have developed into a confident woman, and I want to empower other people to be more successful and happier through positive thinking. I strive to become the best possible version of myself through continual learning and helping other people become the best possible version of themselves. I want to travel the world, see different cultures, learn from them, and be able to work for myself in my NM business.

It is all about the right mindset, and you can achieve anything you dream of. It is important to have big dreams, so you have something to work towards. Our thinking influences our feelings, and happiness releases energy that gets us moving and working.

I have started to reprogram my mind with positive thoughts. I have daily habits and routines that help me a lot during this process. You have to do things that you are not comfortable with so you can improve and learn how to deal with certain situations. Getting out of your comfort zone is very important in order to change and learn. Standing still and always doing the same thing is deadly; it's a dream killer.

Life is like walking up a staircase while looking down. We climb on each individual step without knowing when it will end. But all of a sudden, there is a moment when a platform appears, having waited for us, showing us the next set of stairs. These platforms, with their challenges, make sense. They prepare us for the next level. Each level has its difficulties. Without mastering one level, we won't be strong enough for the next level, and we will not get any further. We cannot avoid defeat; it is part of life and business.

A person's success is not to be judged according to what he achieves in life but the obstacles he overcame on the way to success.

BIOGRAPHY

Claudia Pugl is a world traveller and adventurer. After finishing her schooling in Germany, she attended a year of high school in the USA in LA County to improve her English skills. Back in Germany, she was a trainee painter and decorator and also worked in a theatre in Hamburg. Her passion for travelling and her urge for adventure led her to work in foreign countries such as the Netherlands (six years) and Austria (five years). She currently resides in South Germany, focusing on building her online business and helping other people to live life on their own terms with more happiness and confidence. She enjoys outdoor sports such as skiing in the winter and hiking in the summer.

Connect with Claudia Pugl via https://linktr.ee/Beccy220

CHAPTER 8

Leadership After The 1st Million . . . In The Fourth Quarter Of Life

By David Velasquez

Leadership drives success. There are many definitions of success; it means something different for everyone. Many measure success in terms of amassing financial freedom and time freedom. I did that based on good luck, good skills, and great leadership. I've been most successful when I've had good leadership and when I've been a good team leader. I don't see myself as a great leader, but I have always surrounded myself with great leaders, mentors, and role models. Leaders demonstrate courage, knowledge, competency, and an ability to listen better than their protégés. The Army teaches, "Leadership is the process of influencing people by providing purpose, direction, and motivation while operating to accomplish the mission and improving the organization."[10] Leaders take measured risks on their own but are generally more risk-averse and prudent with others. Once you've benefited from great leadership, you always seek it, and you miss it when it's gone.

---

10 "ADP 6-22 Army Leadership - Caccapl.blob.core.usgovcloudapi.net," accessed November 24, 2021, https://caccapl.blob.core.usgovcloudapi.net/web/repository/doctrine/adp-6-22.pdf.

But if you grew up like me, you believe making money provides for everything you need for your family and legacy. It does not. But it certainly makes everything easier. How does life change after the first million dollars? How do you feel purposeful and motivated to demonstrate *Impact Leadership* when you're free from the classic constraints of money, career, and responsibilities towards parents and children/grandchildren in the fourth quarter of life?

For those who don't know me and my wife of thirty years, Teresa, and missed our story on the first million dollars I authored in 2012 in *The Art and Science of Success, Volume II*, here's a summary.

Today, we live semi-retired in my hometown of San Antonio, Texas. We grew up very modest, so it was easy to always live below our means and save for the future. I worked through college at the local grocery chain, HEB, graduating from Trinity University with a BS in Electronics Engineering and an Army Officer commission in 1981. I had the best co-workers at HEB and the best roommate in college. And I survived a near-fatal car accident.

I worked for the best leaders in the Army. Most retired as three-star Generals, and Col. Bill Guerra taught me to work hard, play hard, and have fun. I got promoted ahead of others and was blessed to lead technical work on the challenging modernization issues of the eighties and nineties. There is no better leadership experience than military service. I served in high-tech areas across the USA and Germany. I went to grad school twice. I graduated from the Naval Postgraduate School with a degree in systems technology. I received a Master of Military Arts and Sciences degree from the Army Command and Staff College. I survived a broken neck in 1987 with no paralysis but retired early in 1996, after fifteen years.

On transition, I went to work for a lowkey mid-sized ($3B) defense contractor. I led technical teams in command and control, modeling and simulation, and cyber security—all technical disciplines.

That company became the nation's largest ($10B, 50,000 employees) employee-owned high-tech company, then the largest stock market IPO behind Mastercard in 2006. Between that windfall and an Army Officer pension, we went millionaire that year at the age of forty-eight. I learned much from several technical and business leaders and retired from that career after sixteen years in 2012. Teresa had "retired" early after a corporate windfall, then downsizing in 2008. That freedom gave us time to think about what we wanted to do with the rest of our lives. We never put our arms around a vision of what to do next. We helped raise our grandson, RJ—he's the best. We helped care for my very independent parents through their passing in 2018 and 2019, and today, we still help Teresa's mom. And we help my awesome flight attendant/pilot daughter to success-orient her parental career and personal passions.

On the side (and it's so important to use your spare time to grow), I volunteered for the board at my local credit union for twenty years, starting in 2000. The credit union mission balanced savers and borrowers to help underserved members of modest means grow a secure future. My first CEO encouraged me, and I earned an MBA in 2004 to better serve the members. The credit union went national, grew to $3B, and I learned strategic leadership from top business leaders, in-house and nationwide. Similarly, an MBA classmate introduced me to network marketing in 2010. I traveled the world and achieved the top 0.09% income earner success by helping hundreds of friends earn their success. I learned lifelong leadership lessons from the very best in that $189B industry. Through network marketing, I met several wealthy and trustworthy real estate private lenders. They included my investments into their efforts, similar to the credit union mission, to help fund typical renters to become homeowners. Perhaps not so ironically, the blending of the credit union mission and values training, the network marketing ideals, and my subsequent real estate investment business helped form my values and vision in the fourth quarter of life.

We know nowadays that anyone can go millionaire if they start young and invest routinely. We tripled our wealth over the next fifteen years through 2020, and we see the magic of compounding interest—and all our efforts—at least doubling that wealth again in the fourth quarter of life. We are so grateful for all the lessons and results on that journey. But, so what, right? So, what is next?

Who would have foreseen a deadly pandemic in 2020 and an erratic 2021 recovery, characterized by the highest inflation in many years, supply chain shortages, and large and small business and school closures, amongst the craziest, most divisive political climate? The lockdowns nearly devastated my network marketing side business, and more so, challenged my passion for it. For many, that big lead they had going into the fourth quarter shrunk. I believe that despite all that success, I made that typical small business entrepreneur mistake, thinking too small and slowing too soon. Why do we not go further and faster when we have momentum?

I became complacent in celebrating the little things: daily wake-ups and feeling *mostly* fulfilled, sharing life, and ensuring the peace of mind of my wife, my daughter, and RJ, my grandson. Proverbs 13:22 says, "A good man leaves an inheritance to his children's children . . ." I got excited living off the compounding interest and monthly market gains (agonized losses), keeping routine social media connections with friends made over a lifetime (mourned all the deaths we witnessed), and achieving the annual Delta Medallion and Southwest A-List status—silly, and fairly selfish. I am very grateful, but I often feel there is much more to accomplish, much more time to do more. Napoleon Hill tells us, "It takes half your life before you discover life is a do-it-yourself project."[11] I, therefore, continued working on myself and my mindset,

---

11 "Napoleon Hill Quotes," BrainyQuote (Xplore), accessed November 24, 2021, https://www.brainyquote.com/quotes/napoleon_hill_384677.

staying connected and reading and watching the classic leaders in my networks, especially those not yet in the fourth quarter.

While my clan will be okay post-pandemic (still talking *a few million*), I realized, as a leader, that your life has almost nothing to do with you. It is more about everyone whose life you touch. My daughter, Veronica, is motivated about career and finances. Steve, my new son-in-law, is wise, and we have instilled key values in my grandson, RJ. I hope I can further positively influence and educate RJ. I want to have an impact like my father did with me. RJ is nine years old now and beginning to understand our past successes, and thus, I've dedicated this book to him for his future use. Teresa and I try to educate him through casual responses like we 'do our businesses for work.' He knows we 'do the stock market,' and we 'let the money we saved make money so we don't have to work a job and can be home with you more,' and he is 'happy to spend time with Grandpa and Grandma.' I loved giving my parents a lot of time for several years before they passed in 2018, 2019, and RJ was often with me, especially on #BarbacoaSundays. RJ has recently started to echo those concepts back to me. So, it's sticking.

So after over a year of self-reflection, counting our blessings, and observation during COVID-19 restrictions, I found my influence on others dissipated and was almost negligible. I'd been fairly lazy—in a comfort zone. And while that was living a good life, it was not good enough. Again, I was thinking too small.

Ron Kaufman tells us, "Never rest on past success. Create something better."[12] But what should I do? What would I create, given so many options? Opportunities abound. I am skeptical and shy away from many of the 'deals' offered, especially if it sounds time-consuming, risky, or only self-serving. I'm flooded with job offers, all of which are rather uninteresting to me. My close friend Rhonda Chase, whom I've

---

12   "Ron Kaufman Quote," A, accessed November 24, 2021, https://www.azquotes. com/quote/1198538.

always admired, hinted early in the pandemic that "most [people] seem more concerned for their 401k than the 400k+ dead from the pandemic or the millions out of work. We have much to face in the years to come. Our unquenched consumption without concern for sustainable living will have to change!" So, I think the sustainability issue moved me to go solar at home and buy more Tesla stock that can grow to pay for my conversion to electric vehicles. But the sustainability challenge did not inspire me to lead the change. Then, there's an Ethereum mining opportunity under formulation, and that's great, but I don't see that investment as a leadership challenge to help others. So, I stay open-minded, participating in several interest groups to narrow down an area of passion to dive into—real estate investors, stock market investors, Veteran entrepreneurs, network marketing, self-development, and various alumni groups. I even seriously considered political office but decided to avoid that negative environment, and so lost before I even started.

I'm still evolving my "Why" for the fourth quarter, or at least, that has been my excuse for lack of activity lately. But the truth is, I am confident whatever direction inspires us, we will leave things in a better state than we found them. My value proposition is that I am an expert, an authority. We've figured out how to be fairly successful in many areas and how to lead others to success.

The leadership imperatives are the same:

- Just decide to take action. Remember that the past doesn't determine the future.
- Stay healthy. Keep learning. But play harder.
- Surround yourself with a leadership team or a mastermind group. It drives accountability.
- Belief and desire are a given. Evolve and commit to a vision.

- Make some goals. Take action persistently. Track results.

- Master the fundamentals. Be the leader who sets the bar.

- Activity drives results. Results attract winners. Winners help others WIN.

Help others WIN to multiply your effort—similar to compound interest and monthly market gains.

For 2022 and beyond, I'm committed to:

1. Experiencing more fun and joy with family and friends than I ever have;

2. Being healthy and improving my life so I can help more people WIN than before;

3. Learning and growing more to leverage the opportunities before me.

I have time and plan to WIN another round but have *only* the fourth quarter. Zig Ziglar teaches, "You can have everything in life you want, if you will just help enough other people get what they want."[13] I will be purposeful in my service. I realize my purpose is to use my gifts and the many skills and experiences I've gained to help other people get what they want. RJ knows there are no limits to what he can accomplish. Hopefully, he and others are a big part of this. That is where I will demonstrate *Impact Leadership* in the fourth quarter of life.

---

13 "Zig Ziglar Quotes," BrainyQuote (Xplore), accessed November 24, 2021, https://www.brainyquote.com/quotes/zig_ziglar_381984.

BIOGRAPHY

David Velasquez is an entrepreneur, investor, and co-author of the 2012 best-seller, *The Art and Science of Success, Vol II*. After admirable success through his midlife, he offers leadership challenges of thinking BIG in the fourth quarter of his life. He is a seasoned leader with an impressive education and diverse experiences as a retired Army officer, a retired high-tech Fortune 300 manager, and a former federal credit union board director of twenty years. A lifelong learner, he has a BS in electronics engineering and three master's degrees, including an Executive MBA and a lifetime of formal professional military and corporate and network marketing leadership training. Having fun living life in his comfort zone, David operates his two businesses, mentors proteges, and mostly serves as the one and only "Abuelo" for his grandson, RJ. A proud father and grandfather, he and his wife, Teresa, travel in a financial, social network with family and friends.

Connect with David Velasquez via https://linktr.ee/DavidSVelasquez

CHAPTER 9

Feed The Faith, Fight The Fear

By Edson Richards, CPA

As a young man, I always wondered what made great people great. What made some people so courageous and others so fearful? Why were some so rich, yet others could scarcely get by? Why did it seem that some could get whatever they wanted, and others kept struggling from day to day? I wondered how Martin Luther King Jr. was able to be so bold during the civil rights era despite the fierce opposition he and many others faced. I grappled with the thought of Noah building the Ark even though it had never rained on the earth before. I asked myself, what trait made Mahatma Gandhi, despite the odds, lead a successful nonviolent campaign for India's independence from British rule? How did Oprah Winfrey become a household name, a media mogul, and a cultural icon despite suffering many awful challenges as a child? These and other questions led me to ponder over life, and particularly my own.

Now, having had some wins and losses playing at the game of life, and through my own personal study, I've come to understand that the one thing all great, successful men and women have in common is faith. Much has been spoken and written about faith. The Bible describes faith this way: "[F]aith is the substance of things hoped for, the evidence of things not seen" (Hebrews 11:1 KJV). Some people describe it as being able to see the invisible, while others say there's no such thing as faith at all. Yet, some say the only *faith* that exists is the *fate* we are destined to live out based on our country of birth, our parents, the amount of money we inherited, and so on. So, is there any truth to this powerful emotion called faith? Is it real, and how do you know if you possess it? Well, I want to tell you that we all possess it. It is an internal gift waiting to be activated, and it cannot be taken away from you because it is internal. Thus, it cannot simply be given away either. Therefore, only you can control this gift and use it to assist you in overcoming your obstacles. If you are determined to break from the past and thrust yourself into your future, to become the leader you were destined to be, then you must exercise your faith. However, in order to do that, you ought to know what faith is and what it is not.

Now, I don't know about you, but for me, one of the most frustrating things people told me when I was going through a difficult time is to "Have faith…everything is going to be alright." What did they really mean when they threw out the cliché, "have faith"? I know these people meant well, and those words may be comforting to others. But for me, I've learned that everything doesn't just work out because you want it to. My experience informs me that if you are going through a tough time and you are looking to get lasting behavioral changes and their corresponding results, you must respond with a clear plan of action to lead your way back. You cannot simply accept life's fate. But it's necessary that you respond by activating your faith, or as I like to call this process, *feeding your faith*. So, what is this thing called faith? Here's my simple definition. Faith is action; faith is *belief* in action! Faith is **believing** that the **actions** you take will result in the desired and expected outcome. One writer says, "[F]aith without works is dead" (James 2:20 KJV). Here is another way to put it: Your faith is proven by your actions. This is why a farmer who believes in his harvest plants his seeds. He is confident that his correct actions will result in that harvest. So, are you feeding your faith, or are you living in fear?

Now, there was a time in my life when I became truly fearful. Before that time, I had achieved something I had always wanted. I had started a business after leaving behind a successful professional career. For the following five years, my business afforded me to vacation several times a year. I had the autonomy I wanted, and I was getting paid! Soon after, that business dried up within a very short span of time, and I was quickly out of money. I became extremely down about myself, I felt like a failure, and that paralyzing emotion called fear crept into my life. Fast forward to today, life is going very well as I once again own and operate my own business, and the future is looking bright.

So, how was I able to bounce back? How was I able to regain my confidence and get my life back on the right track after suffering much defeat? The answer: I had to activate my faith. I had to start believing that there was more to life than what I was currently experiencing. So, I began to implement a series of steps that, over time, righted my mind (my thinking) and catapulted me back on the road to success. Before I share these simple steps with you, I believe it is necessary for me to tell you more about my desert experience after that failed business.

After my money and friends vanished, and I couldn't get a job because of my immigration status, I stopped believing in myself. I had lost my way and truly disengaged my faith; I became very timid. Now, this is not a story where I tell you that I started to use drugs, drink alcohol excessively, or anything like that. But I became so fearful of trying that it had a crippling effect on me as those two vices can. I was concerned about what people thought about me and became so terribly negative that I couldn't see past my failure.

Sharing some of these details of my life's journey is difficult for me as I am a very private person. However, I'm peeling back the onion of my past because I believe that if you are caught in a bad situation like I was, you need to revisit or reflect on your past behavior to understand why you lost your way in the first place. That is, you must strive for **self-awareness**. This was a very painful experience for me, and perhaps it will be for you as well. But trust me, the "look-back" will be well worth it. Just like a car stuck in a very tight parking space, you might have to back up a few times before you can fully move forward. So, do not think this is a one-hour exercise to be rushed through. This may take you some time, as it did for me.

Upon reflecting, I realized that there were some flaws in my thinking, and we all suffer from these blind spots to varying degrees. When things are going well in life, those blind spots or weaknesses are often hidden, and you may not know that you have them. For example, sometimes, you do not know you have an addiction until you attempt to stop drinking or try to reduce your time watching television. Up to the point of my business failure, I had never really had any experience of failure: I always did well in school; I went to college and earned a four-year degree in three years: I landed the career job I wanted in my first interview, etc.

My life up to then could be described as being easy. I never had a tough personal situation to overcome where I had to dig deep to find the solution and face the real me. Sometimes, life's challenges will "strip you down" to reveal your authentic self before you can be introduced to your glorious future ahead. God asked Adam, "Where are you?" (Genesis 3:9 KJV). That rhetorical question was not for God to discover where Adam was, but for Adam's self-awareness. He needed to recognize the mess he was in and reflect on how he had gotten there. Likewise, I'm asking you: Do you know where you are at this stage of your life's journey? Are you living out your dreams? Are you stuck with a job you don't like because you need the benefits and the paycheck? Are you in a toxic relationship from which you can't muster the strength to break? Are you living paycheck to paycheck, unable to stand the feeling of having to constantly sacrifice your needs and wants? Here is the big one. Do you live in a state of unforgiveness because someone hurt you, or did you do something wrong, and you are struggling to forgive yourself because of the hurt you've caused?

To break out of these or any difficult situations, you will need to revisit the past to determine how you ended up in your current situation. I know this may be very painful to do, but it is necessary to assess your past and current situations so you can move forward towards a brighter future for yourself. Otherwise, much like a beautiful woman who always finds herself in an abusive relationship, you may be prone to repeat past mistakes and bad decisions. How does she always attract "that" kind of guy? Is she the problem, or are the men the problem? I don't know. What I do know is that in all those relationships, she was the common denominator. There is something within her thought process that needs healing. And for her—as it is for any of us—to heal, we need to know what's wrong. To know what's wrong, we have to diagnose. And like a good doctor, to diagnose, we must ask questions. Some of these questions can be routine, and some can be extremely uncomfortable. And in bad situations, we may be required to get undressed, and even worse, be rushed into surgery to get the help we need.

Therefore, I decided to face myself and went into deep surgery on my mind. As a result, I learned that one of the precious gifts human beings possess is that we can be our own physicians, our own guides in starting the work of healing our minds to change our course towards the path of happiness and fulfillment. The first thing I'll ask you to do is to forgive, forgive, forgive. Forgive everyone who has ever emotionally hurt you, lied to you, cheated on you, stole from you, deceived you, or physically hurt you. Forgive them all. However, most of all, **forgive yourself.** Yes, forgive yourself, and do not play the victim or the blame game any longer.

Remember when God spoke to Adam after he had done something he wasn't supposed to? Do you know what Adam did next? He blamed Eve. And Eve, in turn, blamed the serpent. Neither of them took any responsibility. Of course, I'm not saying that if someone lied to you or stole from you that you are responsible for it. However, if you continue to harbor negative emotions towards that person, that will only hurt you, not the perpetrator. You are giving this person your power! So, the first thing I'll ask you to do is forgive the offender for the pain inflicted on you. That doesn't mean you forget about the incident; it just means it no longer reigns any power over you. Conversely, you may have wronged others as well. Don't wait for them to forgive you. Forgive yourself immediately so you can move on. Apologize if you can. Make amends where you can. But let no one hold you to your past actions. We are all evolving, so don't allow your former self to stop you from becoming the best version of you.

So, now that we've gotten forgiveness out of the way, and you've decided to release those negative emotions towards yourself and others, let me give you my steps to feeding the faith that will catapult you towards impactful leadership.

Step One. You must design a clear written vision of the person you will become and the type of lifestyle that accompanies that. You should define success on your terms. Who will you be? Where will you go? What impact will you have on society? I've heard a great man say: Success is to make what you see on the inside become what you see on the outside. Hence, this vision must be yours and not someone else's. Start by assessing the gifts and talents you possess. Ask your trusted family, friends, and associates what strengths and competencies they think you possess. Candidly ask them how they "see you," and don't be offended by their answers. Also, consider taking a personality test to determine your possible areas of interest. However, the key to forming your vision is to invest time alone with yourself to think about your life in silence. *You must disconnect from the world in order to connect with yourself.* Quieting your mind will give you what you are seeking. I promise you . . . this process works. **Do not** overlook this step! You must get alone with yourself for an hour, or two, or three, or however long it takes. Then, as you think about who you will become, write down what comes to mind as your inner voice aids you in crafting that vision. I have completed this amazing process and was shocked by what was revealed to me. I promise you'll be amazed by this process as well.

Step Two. Once you've clearly established your vision, you should set specific, time-based goals to get and keep you on track with your vision. Like your vision, these must be written down. Simply put, successful people know where they are going, and they use time-based, measurable goals to assist them in getting to their destination. If your target is unclear, it will be very difficult to measure your achievement. Therefore, create time-based, measurable goals that you'll track (daily, weekly, etc.) to determine if you are on target with realizing your vision. Caution: Set goals that are believable and achievable for you. Don't try to go from zero to hero! I suggest using a concept called *SMART* goal setting, which you can explore more online.

Step Three. Begin to build your faith around your vision and goals. You do this by reading them out loud every day. "[F]aith cometh by hearing, and hearing by the word" (Romans 10:17 KJV). Also, you must find pictures that reflect the accomplishment of your vision and goals. This creative process is called dream building. Put these pictures on your phone, on your computers, in your car, and in your home, any place where you can see them daily. As you read your goals and see the pictures, imagine them as already achieved, and see yourself in them. This is a key point because you'll only achieve what you constantly see in your mind. And if you see examples of your achievement often enough, it will develop within you a strong desire to possess them so that you can continually execute the next step.

Step Four. Finally, here comes the most important step in this process. You are required to go to work; you must apply action! You should develop a written, defined plan of action steps that you will execute daily. These action steps must be scheduled in your calendar as part of your daily activity. My philosophy is this: *If it is not scheduled, then it's not real!* That is, you must build a daily routine as there is no substitute for doing the predetermined work. When you begin to see the small achievements towards your goals, those same achievements will fuel you to take even more actions towards your goals. This is one of the reasons why your goals need to be measurable.

Now, let's spend a little time talking about the major reason most people never get started on their dreams . . . **fear**! There are different types of fear, and they can all be as crippling to you as Kryptonite is to Superman. I have no doubt that there is a **Superman** or **Superwoman** inside you. However, for most of us, our fears stop us from getting out of the starting block and into the race of life. The best thing about this race is that it is your own. You are not competing against anyone as it relates to living out **your** vision for your life. That's right, there's no one to your right or left challenging you. You decide if you win in life or lose. To win, you must overcome your fears by making cold, calculated decisions to do the work in any way, despite being fearful. This requires an act of your will, or as I've coined it, *fighting the fear*. Consistently developing the habit of doing the work despite being fearful is the only true way to fight through your fears. I'm sure you've heard this definition of **FEAR**: False Evidence Appearing Real. That means fear is only a state of mind. Therefore, **YOU** can shift **YOUR** state of mind by implementing the steps noted above. So don't get faked out. Make a decision to run through that imaginary barrier that's holding you back because your victory is on the other side.

In summary, feeding your faith through the steps noted above while overcoming your fears through planned, decisive actions is a sure way to get you on the road leading to your dreams. It's also helpful to get assistance from others. Find a mentor or someone qualified to aid you in your endeavors. Glean wisdom from them and use their experiences to help you along the way. My last tip is for you to adopt some mantra for living. I repeat this phrase over and over to myself whenever I'm facing a difficult time: *Feed the faith, fight the fear! Feed the faith, fight the fear! Feed the faith, fight the fear!* Repeating these words always steadies my mind, and I hope it does for you as well.

Get excited! There's a brand-new coming attraction, and that's you! Welcome to *Impact Leadership* and here's to your success . . . Cheers!

BIOGRAPHY

Edson Richards, CPA, has a career in business spanning over fifteen years. Edson was born on the beautiful Caribbean Island of Antigua and moved to the United States to pursue higher education. After earning a BA in Accounting, Edson worked for two of the largest public accounting firms. There, he obtained his license as a Certified Public Accountant while working on audits for many large public and private firms. He is currently the owner and CEO of Blueprint Financial Services LLC, a firm specializing in individual and corporate accounting and tax. Edson loves to help others and is a teacher at heart. His purpose is to teach others how to take charge of their minds so that they can live richer, more fulfilled lives. He loves reading, traveling to new places, and is always up for a great personal growth seminar. Edson resides in Dallas with his wife and two beautiful daughters.

Connect with Edson Richards via https://linktr.ee/erichards

CHAPTER 10

Overcoming A Monster

By Felix Figueroa Jr.

Have you ever been in a deep sleep and heard someone telling you to wake up? 'Wake up! Hey, wake up! You need to get up now!' And then, you open your eyes, and there's no one there. It has happened to me, but I wasn't waking up from a deep sleep. I was waking up from a heroin overdose, and the needle was still in my arm as I was trying to come to my senses and get up from my bathroom floor.

Only God knows how long I was lying on my bathroom floor. The only thing I know is that it was early afternoon when I shot myself with dope, and it was late at night when God woke me up. He said He had a plan for me. At that moment, I didn't know what the plan was, but I didn't care. What I certainly knew was that I didn't want to die.

It wasn't always like this. I grew up a normal kid in a safe environment, with two older sisters and amazing parents. My father was the provider, and my mother was a housewife. He always worked hard to make sure we had what we needed. We lived in a nice neighborhood. Growing up, I remember we'd all set the table for dinner every evening. We also had movie nights. We used to have a Bible study as a family once a week, and we also went to church twice a week. My mother and I were very close; I used to tell her everything that went on in my life.

Yes, I was a mama's boy. I was her little angel, even when I was out of my mind, doing street stuff. I also remember being a skinny little boy who was afraid of his own shadow. My two older sisters used to defend me from the school bullies because I didn't have the courage to stand up for myself.

In the eighth grade, I was introduced to marijuana, and something happened. That little skinny boy wasn't afraid anymore. For some reason, drugs gave me the courage I thought I didn't have within me. I was searching for something, and I thought I had found it in drugs. And soon, when I tried heroin, it was like I awoke a monster. From that point on, everything changed. I became rebellious towards my parents and teachers. Deep down inside, I knew that I wanted to seek good things for myself, but I didn't know how. I was young, immature, and in desperate need of some direction. So, I looked up to the big drug dealers who lived in our neighborhood. They had the nicest house and cars. They used to pay me $40 and give me an ounce of weed for cleaning their cars. In the early eighties, that was good money. I also sold weed in school.

As I went on to try different drugs and hang out late and over the weekend with friends, I thought that I was living the life and wanted to try it all. I was in the ninth grade and selling loose joints in school like I had a license to do so. I got expelled a year later.

I now understand that I always wanted to become an entrepreneur, but I chose the wrong product. And, of course, I did tell my parents that the marijuana wasn't mine when we were at the police station and that someone put it in my bookbag. I got kicked out of school, and the police captain let me go with a verbal warrant because he saw the agony on my parents' faces; he noticed that they were good parents, and I was a rebellious teenager. I was kicked out in the tenth grade. However, when I turned eighteen, I pursued a GED.

A little after I turned eighteen, my father kicked me out of the house. I'd hate him for a long time for doing that, but I guess he did the right thing at the time. I had no roof over my head, but I didn't care. So, I went to a friend's house and stayed there for a while before moving to New York City.

The Big Apple! I was excited. I got to the Bronx in the spring of 1984, right on 179th and Creston Ave. I stayed with a high school friend for a few months.

I was looking forward to getting a job and doing well for myself. After all, this was the land of opportunity. It didn't take long for reality to start sinking in. I didn't know any English. I remembered telling my tenth-grade English teacher in Puerto Rico, "We don't need that crap over there. You can shove it up your ass." Yes, she kicked me out of the classroom and told me, "You will need this English someday, and you will remember me." Sure enough, there I was, trying to get a job and didn't know what they were asking me in the interview. But instead of going to school to take some English classes and trying to do the right thing, I took the easy way out, going back to that limited thinking—back in that box. I went and bought a half-pound of weed and started selling it in the parks all over the city (wherever they had live music playing). I would hold the joints in my hands, showing half of them and walking around, calling them loose joints, tabaco suelto, or tabaco suertos. I'd do this as I walked around the park or beach (Coney Island Brighton Beach, or Orchard Beach). I did it all that summer. My dad called one of my cousins living in Sheepshead Bay in Brooklyn at the time. He was a pastry chef. My cousin asked me to move to Brooklyn and offered me a job at the bakery he worked in Queens (a Jewish bakery). So, I moved to Brighton Beach, and I started as a baker's helper. I was excited because I did like to bake, but unfortunately, it didn't last long because of my lack of English proficiency once again.

I later got a job in East New York by New Lots neighborhood, and it didn't require high English proficiency. The only English I needed to know was 'How many?' The job? Selling heroin in the corner. I would work four hours every other day or every day, depending on the demand.

I easily made over $400 in four hours. Easy money, but it went as fast as it came. I truly understood the concept of becoming a product of your product. I became my best customer. I won't get into every detail of my drug abuse, but I will tell you that it took me to places that I thought I would never go.

I remember having a horrible experience with PCP, and I swore to God that I'd never smoke it again. I recall hanging out with my best friend, Raymond, and we were smoking on the number-two train, going uptown to the Bronx from Harlen, where we got the drugs. We were supposed to get off at 149th Street. He got off, but I didn't. I realized that he wasn't on the train until I heard the conductor call for the last stop. I looked around the train and the next car and didn't see him. So, I decided to go back. I remember that it was a weekday, and it was past midnight. When traveling back, the noises from the train were very loud. I was so high that the noises made it feel like my brain was rolling inside my head. So, I got off the train at the next station. I remember it was Chambers Street in Manhattan. The train took off. As I stood there, watching the train leave the station, I peered into the tunnel far away and watched the other train coming in. My only thought—and I was obsessing about it—was to jump in front of the train and stop it. So, I stood right at the edge of the platform and waited for the train. I don't know if you've ever experienced having an idea so bright that nothing would stop you from going through with it. That was me at that moment—standing on that edge of the platform, waiting for the train. The train got closer and closer, and I was getting ready to jump in front of this damn train to stop it when I heard a loud voice: "Don't do it!" I snapped out of it, took two steps back, and looked around. There was nobody in the station: just me . . . and God.

So, as the monster took over my life more and more, I ended up homeless and sleeping on the D-Train or under the boardwalk in Brighton Beach.

I got my first state sentence in 1989. It was on Rikers Island that I heard someone saying in a NA meeting that I didn't have to use drugs ever again. I looked at the guy like he was crazy. Meanwhile, I'd ask the cell block officer to let me out to go to the meeting because I'd want to see if my friend from the other cell block had some dope. At that point, I truly believed that I was going to die getting high.

In 1991, I was on probation in New Jersey for possession of drugs. I got out with the intention of never meeting my probation officer after I got bailed. So, after two felony convictions in New York, one in New Jersey, another one in Puerto Rico, countless detox sessions, and a few outpatient and inpatient rehab sessions, I still went out there to get one more. I didn't know how to stop.

I thought there was something wrong with me because after using to live and living to use for all these years, I still couldn't stop.

It wasn't until I got sick and tired of being sick and tired that I decided to humble myself, seek help, and become teachable. I had to let somebody help me and show me how to live clean because I had forgotten how. I also decided to turn my will and my life over to the care of God: Good Orderly Direction. In NA, I learned how to finally stop using by practicing the principles in The Twelve Steps. I am truly grateful to God for sparing me and taking care of me when I was in the maze. I am also grateful to my NA sponsor for giving me the tools for recovery.

If I can stay clean, so can you. If you are suffering from any type of addiction, the first step is to accept that you have a problem and ask for help. I haven't used any mind-altering substances since December 25, 2008, and my life has changed for the better. I'm finally free from my own self-imprisonment. I have overcome myself. I'm grateful that my mom has the chance to see the transformation in my life before she transitions to the other side.

So, I came to Milwaukee in 2004. Four years later, I got clean and got a job. I wanted to earn more money, and at that point, I made the right decision by enrolling at Milwaukee Area Technical College to study CNC Machines. I met up with a good friend at Starbucks, and he would teach me algebra, geometry, and trigonometry because I needed them to pass the assessment test.

I learned to focus on the solution and not the problem. I'm doing a lot of self-education these days because I want to improve and upgrade my lifestyle. There's always room for improvement. Becoming the best version of myself will take time and dedication; it is a lifetime process. If I can help just one person change and look for help to live life for the purpose they were created, I will be pleased. Thank you, God, for granting me the serenity to accept the things I cannot change, the courage to change the things that I can, and the wisdom to know the difference.

BIOGRAPHY

Felix Figueroa Jr. has been a full-time CNC machinist for the past eleven years and a part-time network marketer. He's working towards becoming a full-time entrepreneur in direct selling and having his own network marketing company. He is an extremely family-oriented, loving, and caring human being. He loves to travel the world—thanks to a secret travel club membership. Being that this is his first book, he would like to dedicate it to his mother. She motivated him to write a book on his past experiences and struggles with drug addiction and how he made it out alive. He hopes that he can help someone to overcome whatever addiction they might be going through.

Connect with Felix Figueroa Jr. via /felix.figueroa.507027

CHAPTER 11

Focus And Achieve

By Hilda Nakhwanga

Has anyone lost their parents in one month? I did, and it would forever be etched in my mind. My parents had attended a family function. Everything had gone well, and everyone was in high spirits, especially my late mother (may her soul rest in peace). But on their way back home, my mother, unfortunately, passed away due to what later was found to be a cardiac arrest. My father had to hold on to her for hours before they could finally arrive at their destination, where my mother's body could be transferred to the morgue. It's unimaginable what went through my father's mind when it occurred to him that my mum had passed away.

Back at home, we were hanging out with friends as we normally did, and we were expecting my parents back that evening. Eventually, when my father got back home, we found it strange that he came back alone. And upon inquiry, he broke the sad news to us. Those were the hardest words I had ever heard in my young adult life, and I was in denial until the point we laid her to rest.

Life had to go on, and it almost felt wrong to go on without her. That whole situation must have hit my father the hardest: he was never himself the days following her burial. He got unwell and was admitted to the hospital for about three days. I remember the evening before he was to be discharged from hospital the following day. We had visited him, and he looked forward to coming home. But it was not to be. And that's how we went through the mourning process in a span of one month. My parents were the people closest to me, and living without them created a big void in my life. There is a certain way parents cushion the family, and when they are gone, you get a feeling of bareness and being exposed without anyone having your back. But on the flip side, the whole experience taught me to be strong and determined in life.

Two days after my father's burial, I had to attend a job interview, and it was apparently being slotted for the second time. The first time was when I had just lost my mother, and the person who received the telephone call in the house did not convey the message to me. I would like to imagine they must have decided I was not in a position to attend the interview—and they were right. As you can imagine, I was still numb and grieving from what had just happened, but I still believed in attending this second interview. The interview went well, but somewhere along the way, the question of why I did not attend the first interview came up. When answering the question, the feelings of sadness came back again, and it was clear that I could not go on with the interview. And so, the interview had to end unceremoniously, so to speak. I felt like I had dropped the ball when I walked out of that boardroom. It felt like I had just let an opportunity slip through my fingers.

But about two weeks later, I was called to start my new job, for which I worked ten years at the top public university in my country. I quickly realized that there was room for upward mobility in my career, and in my quest to succeed, I embarked on a plan to improve my skills by attending evening classes after work. In a span of five years, I had reached a top position. Coming from a patriarchal society, inheriting anything from your parents as a female was an uphill task. So, I worked with what I had—and in this case, education. I thank my parents for educating me. Ten years is a good amount of time to work with an organization, and I eventually felt like I needed a change.

So, I embarked on a job hunt and even sent out unsolicited applications to my dream organizations. I also included friends in my job hunt to alert me of any opportunities in my line of work that they would come across. I attended several interviews without success until I landed on an advert the night before its closing date. The following day, I was in a frenzy of activity, trying to put everything together and submit my application before the deadline. There was no option for online submission at that time, so I had to hand-deliver the application. I went back to my job hunting and totally forgot about this application because they had indicated that if I didn't hear from them in two weeks, it was because the application was unsuccessful.

So, when I got a call to an interview for this position a month later, I realized that it had completely slipped my mind. I went for the interview two days later and got the job.

It was a hectic job that included a bit of travelling, but I still continued pursuing self-development, attending class after work, and earning a degree. It was a challenging feat to balance work, school, and family, considering I had a teenage son in high school at the same time.

The strain on time and finances was quite enormous. But where there is a will, there is a way!

During this time, I had a health scare that, unfortunately, many doctors were not able to diagnose immediately. This condition would leave me exhausted for no apparent reason. So, I rested more than I did anything because I would get out of breath even though I was not overweight. In fact, I had lost quite a bit of weight due to this condition because it affected my metabolism as well. After several visits to the same hospital, I decided to go to another hospital altogether. After the tests had been done, including an electrocardiogram (ECG), I was sent to a heart specialist. After a heart scan and several other tests, he showed me results that indicated a normal heart cavity. The doctor was just as perplexed at my abnormally high heart rate and exhaustion.

Keep in mind that all the other tests had come back normal. The only thing that came to the doctor's mind was to check my thyroxine levels. And when the test was done, we finally found the culprit of my many months of being sick. I looked perfectly fine on the outside until I exerted any effort to carry out a task. Then, the abnormal heart rate and exhaustion kicked in. I did not have physical signs like a goitre (swelling on the neck), and one would therefore not suspect that I had a problem with my thyroid glands.

The cardiologist immediately put me on treatment to reduce my thyroxine levels. My body was overproducing thyroxine (this is known as hyperthyroidism). This happens when your thyroxine glands produce more thyroxine than your body needs. And because it's hormonal, it causes havoc in your body. I continued with treatment for over two years with bi-weekly visits to the endocrinologist (a doctor specializing in endocrine conditions, including thyroid dysfunction). I eventually had to stop the treatment after one of my visits to the doctor indicated that I was getting some serious side effects from the tablets I was taking.

Strangely enough, the tablets, being that they were steroids, were fighting my red blood cells. While, on the other hand, my thyroxine levels were going down. I had to stop taking medicine immediately, and I had a window of two weeks to see whether my thyroxine levels would go up without the medicine. If that would have happened, then I'd have to go through surgery. The surgery would involve cutting the sides of my neck (since the thyroid glands sit on the sides of the neck just below the jaws). This would allow the surgeon to cut off a bit of the glands so that they could produce less thyroxine. Or if worse came to worst, they would altogether remove my thyroid glands, and I would have to live on thyroxine medicine for the rest of my life. And yes, the thought of having someone cutting any part of my neck made me shudder!

I prayed hard for my thyroxine levels to continue going down without the medicine so that I wouldn't have to go through the surgery. Having gone through another major surgery before for an unrelated issue, I was not mentally prepared for another one. And after two weeks, the test indicated that my thyroxine levels were going down and continued to improve. They got back to normal without medication. I haven't had any problems with my thyroid gland up to this day. I also learned at that time that this condition was not very common. That was probably why it wasn't diagnosed quickly.

Once I got well, I embarked on earning my degree, and I went to school after work to make it happen. My job keeps me busy, and part of it includes a bit of travelling. I would be late to class many times because something important came up in the office. It was a challenging time, trying to balance everything, but I had to find a way to make it work.

As I said earlier, I had to grapple with the financial strain. But as they say: Where there is a will, there is a way!

Going through all this as a single parent can be overwhelming at times, especially when you do not have close family members to lean on. Having lost my parents in my early twenties and losing my three siblings in the years that followed made me more empathetic toward single parents. The saying, 'The wearer knows where the shoe pinches most,' is very glaring when you are a single parent. Things that look normal to the outside world could be significantly different for a single parent. I learned to make friends with people I could fully trust to do things for me that involved my child when it was not possible for me to do it. I also learned that balancing your life is not as easy as people make it sound. But living a full life and following your dreams is extremely important.

I have gone ahead to see my son through university, and I have taken in my orphaned niece, who is also currently in university. Seeing them transform to be the best versions of themselves brings joy to me, and this is something that we should all aspire to as humans.

I know this journey called life can beat us left, right, and centre at times, but what's important is that we pick ourselves up and move forward with our heads held up high!

Success is a journey, and it's through our failures that we learn to do better the next time. Always follow your dreams because you do not know when things will change for the better; it could be as close as a razor's edge. So, focus on and achieve what you want.

Does all this mean that I have become successful? It depends on your definition of success. As I said earlier, success is a journey.

Know what your journey is, and know what you want because we learn from life every day. Learn from successful people, and choose what to apply to your life.

And just to quote one famous author, John Maxwell, "Successful and unsuccessful people do not vary greatly in their abilities. They vary in their desires to reach their potential."[14]

So, learn to pick yourself up and push towards your goals. By all means, life is still good, despite the challenges.

---

14 "Successful and Unsuccessful People Do Not Vary Greatly in Their Abilities. They Vary in Their Desires to Reach Their Potential. - John C. Maxwell," Quotespedia. org, April 9, 2020, https://www.quotespedia.org/authors/j/john-c-maxwell/ successful-and-unsuccessful-people-do-not-vary-greatly-in-their-abilities-they-vary-in-their-desires-to-reach-their-potential-john-c-maxwell/.

BIOGRAPHY

Hilda Nakhwanga has a background in media and public relations and has spent most of her career in public diplomacy work. Hilda believes in self-development not just for herself but also for the people around her. She gets satisfaction in being part of their positive transformations. As a person who is always in learning mode, Hilda considers herself a lifelong student and loves to read or listen to experts as they discuss different topics. Hilda is a single parent of a young adult son and her orphaned niece. To relax, Hilda loves to travel and listen to music in her spare time. Her favourite quote on success is by John Maxwell: "Successful and unsuccessful people do not vary greatly in their abilities. They vary in their desire to reach their potential."

Connect with Hilda Nakhwanga via https://linktr.ee/HildaNakhwanga

CHAPTER 12

You Can't Lose, And Even When You Fail, You Win

By James Williams

Hello, and thank you for your interest in reading my book. Pleased to meet you. My story is not one of hard luck, nor am I someone who hit rock bottom only to rise above and become successful. Nevertheless, I would like to share with you some ideas and concepts that may help you now and in the future.

Let's start at the beginning. I grew up in a middle-class family in the Midwest (Milwaukee, WI, to be exact). I am the middle sibling of two brothers and a sister. I had a mother from the South who taught her children to be kind and caring and to step in and help anyone who needed help and serve others. My father was from the North. He taught us to not only be book smart but street smart and to never let anyone take advantage of us. So, I had the best of both worlds. Take these two philosophies and value systems and put them together. And what did I have? I believe I had a very good start. I have always loved reading books and educating myself (readers are leaders). I owe my success to my parents and other mentors in my life. What I learned from them—along with my own collection of books, audios, videos, as well as my own development—increased my knowledge of personal and entrepreneurial success. I was close to my father. Being raised in the North, he taught me a great number of things that I just didn't learn in school. My father was quite streetwise and could see things that would happen well in advance and a mile away. As I was growing up, he also showed me what things to do and what not to do. He taught me how to use my common sense, above all, and take life's experiences and learn from them. These experiences developed my manhood and taught me to be a responsible adult. Let's just say that I never learned any of this from a book. All this helped me a great deal in life. As the late great Jim Rohn said, "Formal education will make you a living; self-education will make you a fortune."[15]

That being said, I was close to my mother too, but differently. Let me explain. My mother never really said the words, 'I love you,' often, but she would say things at times that I would think to myself, 'Why would she say something so bad even if it was true?' I guess that was her southern way to get her point across. I knew that she loved me based on a lot of what she would not say: her actions, and more importantly, how she went to work for our family. There is a saying, "All that I am, I owe to my mother." This is so true. My mother, Sonina, worked for the school board. I attended one of the schools where she worked. My behavior was so bad that she said, 'Enough is enough.' During this time, I was out of control. Being the intelligent southern lady she was, my mother put me in a Catholic school even though we were Methodist. It was good that she did because if she had not, there's no telling where I would have ended up. At the time, I guess I was just lost or needed some direction in life that my parents couldn't offer then. So, off I went to the first of two Catholic schools. The first one was a middle school called St. Thomas. It was on the other side of town and had a diverse group

---

15   "Jim Rohn Quotes," BrainyQuote (Xplore), accessed March 1, 2022, https://www. brainyquote.com/quotes/jim_rohn_121282.

of students. This was something I was not used to. But looking back, it was good for me. It gave me the ability to get along and interact with all kinds of people who would help me immensely later in life. The nuns, priest, and the rest of the staff at that school truly cared about me as a person, and I did a 360 in terms of my behavior.

My mother used to smile at me, and I think she knew that sending me to that school was a good move, even though she never really said it out loud. I tried out for the basketball team and became a starter. What made the experience even more life-changing was the coach. He really made an impact on my life. The care I received from the nuns, priest and staff was more than good, but what I received from him was the icing on the cake. He was not only a coach but a friend who taught and showed me things that my father, mother, siblings, and others could not.

I was part of a team that worked so well that we won the title for our division of Catholic schools. I was on top of the world, winning the title. My home and school life were awesome. Life was good and as perfect as it could get. So, I was transformed in just one short year, and everyone, including my parents, could see it.

As graduation approached, I had to think about what high school I was going to enroll in. I thought about it but didn't give it much thought. I was too busy thinking about and enjoying what happened last year. As graduation got closer, I knew I had to make a decision. So, I chose another Catholic school called Messmer. This one was closer to my house. I could even walk or run since I was an athlete. So, over the summer, I thought about the classes I was going to take and what sport (or sports) I would play. When I started high school, I picked out my classes. As far as sports were concerned, I thought to myself, 'Why don't I do what Jim Thorpe did?' So, I played three sports: baseball in the spring, football in the summer, and basketball in the fall and winter.

Two years in, I was in a good place, and everything was going well. Then, I lost my father, and my mother was left to support four children alone. She worked at the school board but had to pick up another job to make ends meet. That led me to grow up fast. My mother, siblings, and friends found a way to make it work. Needless to say, I grew up in an environment that was less than ideal without my father.

It was this environment, the trauma of losing my father and not having him in my life, that led me towards a self-destructive and downward spiral. I found myself in bad company, making bad decisions, and doing things that weren't in my best interest. I was lost for a while. There were days when I only watched TV or did absolutely nothing. I told myself that I had to do something, so I got into books, tapes, and videos on personal development, motivation, and positive affirmations.

It was slow, but I started to believe in myself again and take positive steps to change my life. I did not want my family to struggle (especially my mother). So, I stepped up. I started working temp jobs, doing work that I really did not care for, like working in factories and similar jobs. I thought to myself that things would get better. I leaned on my older brother, Greg, a bit because my father had passed. He helped on many occasions. At times, I did not like him very much, but he had my best interest at heart and meant well. I owe him quite a bit for what he did for me when I really needed him. Later in life, we talked about things I did that slipped my memory. I'm glad we did because it made me revisit and reflect on my past decisions along with my skills and talents, which I had forgotten.

My sister, Nina, whose name was derived from my mother's, was a good sibling. My older brother, Billy, and I fought among ourselves (like many kids do). However, when someone other than family came against us, all I can say is "watch out" because we were a united front against adversaries. Just thinking back gives me great memories: the holidays, trips, cookouts. These were the good times I remember, even when it didn't feel so good. It was the best my mother could provide.

It was later in life when I recalled something my father told me. Something, I believe, is very true of any job you do: "You can make money with your back or your mind. It is your choice." A light bulb immediately went on in my head. Sales!—I needed to get into sales!

I found myself working all kinds of sales-related jobs that involved the phone (call center), direct, retail, and more. I was exposed to some of the industry's best sales and marketing training at some of these jobs. I became really good at selling. I was not the kind of person who would take advantage of a customer but instead help them make the most informed decision based on what they needed or wanted.

When I was working as an assistant manager at a shoe store, I ran into a man who asked me about my current job and what I was looking for in the future. I did not know it then, but he had been watching me for some time. He was a department manager of a high-end furniture, appliance, and electronics retailer. I came to the conclusion he was trying to recruit me. After a brief exchange, he convinced me to take a chance and work for this high-end retailer. I was a bit concerned with working on straight commission. He assured me that he would personally train me and show me everything that I needed to become successful in his department so that working on straight commission with the skills and training that he'd give me would not be an issue at all. So, I told him, "Let's do it!"

After being mentored by him, I very quickly became successful in that sales department. I got to the point where I was moving $250,000–$500,000 a quarter. I was making very good money but had no free time. It seemed like I was always working. There was a guy who worked in the furniture department. He was making $100,000 a year, but he was at work 70–80 hours, seven days a week. I did not want to be on a treadmill like that. People like him eventually burn themselves out or get sick being on a grind like that.

As luck would have it, I got this magazine in the mail one day. There was an African-American gentleman on the cover who looked like me and was someone I could identify with. When I read his bio, I found out that he was making $25,000 per month. I was doing well, but not like that. I thought to myself, 'I need to look at this.' So, I jumped into the direct sales industry with an excellent company.

It went very well for me right from the start due to a great product and service, and it got to the point I was doing so well it was hard for me to go back to work. I started calling in sick quite often and then just ran out of reasons to go. So, I had to decide: keep working that job or take a chance by taking a leave of absence to see if I could do this full-time. Well, that was seventeen years ago, and I have been job-free ever since. That high-end furniture, appliance, and electronics retailer is no longer in business. I have learned that you can always learn something—even in the bad times. When you think about it that way, you've not really lost, you've only gained. That is why I named this chapter "You Can't Lose, and Even When You Fail, You Win."

Now, I own my schedule, and I am able to do whatever I want, whenever I want, without calling in or checking with a boss. I live life on my own terms. It's been truly life-changing for me. I've discovered the secrets to making money online, through social media, and helping those who have yet to discover how to advertise their business using social media. I truly enjoy sharing my strategy with people who truly want to get ahead and go for their dreams. My specialties are helping entrepreneurs begin, jump start, and run a successful business from home and coaching them to make as much money as their hearts desire. I have also expanded what I do to include B2B (business to business). I do this by helping businesses to generate sales on and offline, putting systems in place, and automating those sales in order to protect, fund, and upscale them.

My passions also include helping people, families, and businesses get to the next level and beyond. My mother and father have both passed away. I am truly grateful to them, countless other families, and so many others from whom I've learned so much.

I want to give and be of service to others. Pay it forward so others can do the same. Thank you for your attention, and best of luck to you.

BIOGRAPHY

James Williams has had a career in sales and marketing that spans various companies over the last thirty-plus years. As a result, he is now a twenty-first-century entrepreneur committed to helping individuals, families, and small-to-medium-size companies get to the next level. His passions include spending quality and quantity time with family and friends. He helps improve the lives of others through service, mentorship, giving back to the community, and helping them live lives of purpose so that they too can give back and make this a better world. He currently resides in Milwaukee, WI. He is motivated by a simple saying: "By the yard is hard. However, inch by inch, anything is a cinch." If you have a goal and are willing to work at it, you will succeed because you cannot hit a target you do not have.

Connect with James Williams via https://linktr.ee/jameswilliams360

CHAPTER 13

The Power In, And Believing In, The Name Of Jesus

By Jamie Stewart

"And being found in fashion as a man, he humbled himself and became obedient unto death, even the death of the cross. Wherefore God also hath highly exalted him and given him a name which is above every name: that at the name of Jesus every knee should bow, of things in heaven, and things in earth, and things under the earth; and that every tongue should confess that Jesus Christ is Lord, to the glory of God the Father" (Philippians 2:8-11 KJV).

The power in the name of Jesus and believing in the name of Jesus grew in me when my mother was addicted to drugs (crack, to be specific).

There were times my mother would get so high that she would start sweating like someone threw water on her. Other times, she would be foaming at the mouth, her eyes rolling to the back of her head. By the time she got through calling for me, I'd place her head on my lap as she'd gasp for air. She would say, "Jamie, call my friend." Now, as a young lady at the tender age of eight or nine years, it would have been easy for me to think she was talking about someone she grew up with, worked with, somebody from the neighborhood, or a close cousin. But no. She would be referring to her imaginary friend. As a child, I and the others found the idea of having imaginary friends weird. Like most people's invisible friends, no one finds out about them until the person who created them is unexpectedly found to be interacting with them. So, it was simply strange for my mother, who was an adult, to have an imaginary friend— not only strange but embarrassing at the time. There were times I would be sitting on her lap, and Mom, scratchily gasping for air in her throat with her tongue stuck to the bottom of her mouth, would only have the breath to ask me to call for her imaginary friend as her spit bubbles would pop and splash on my face, landing on my cheeks and below my eyes (luckily never in my eye).

As all this would take place, all I could think of was wishing it would be done with—but healthily. My heart would pump so hard it felt that it was coming out of my chest. I would have no other choice than to scream and cry, 'Mom! Mom!' with my tears and spit all over her. My instincts were telling me to go and look for help, that we needed help, but I would not do this because when I did so before, it would simply make things worse. When my siblings would come to help, they'd tell me, "Get away from Satan!" But this was my mom! She would wrap herself around me very tightly with all her dead weight on me that I could not get her out of my lap. So, my siblings would try to pull me away from her, but her grip on me would be too tight. My sister and brother would yell at my mom, "Let her go, Satan!" Then, a tug of war would ensue. It's amazing how children pick up cues from their environment. The only way I could justify my siblings calling my mother 'Satan' was because that's how bad she looked close to death.

Growing up, we knew a few kids who had invisible/imaginary friends. We thought it was strange and that they were possessed by something. In the case of my mother, she was possessed by drugs. I couldn't even call the police because it would look bad, given that we were one of two African American families on that suburban block. We kids would have been taken away from Child Protective Services (CPS), and we did NOT want that at all.

I remember crying one time as my mother overdosed and called for her imaginary friend. I yelled out, "I DON'T KNOW YOUR FRIEND!" My mom, with a faint voice, said, "Ju . . . Ju . . . Ju . . . Jesus." Then, she went out like a light with her eyes still wide open. You could see nothing but the white of her eyes, and her mouth would be slightly open with her tongue off to the side, just barely hanging out. Her face was damp, and she had no body movement. All I could think at that moment was, 'Mom, I don't know your friend, so here goes nothing.' Then, I cried uncontrollably, "Ju . . . Ju . . . Ju . . . Jesus. My mom told me to call you." I had a vague recollection of my mom telling me that I wouldn't need a phone for her friend, Jesus; I just had to call His name. Calling out for Jesus seemed as scary as calling for Bloody Mary in front of the bathroom mirror. At that point in my life, I knew more about Bloody Mary than I did about Jesus. So, I continued to call out to Him, "Jesus, help my mom. She's your friend. She asked me to call you for help. She passed out again." I called on his name repeatedly. The next thing I knew, it was noon the following day.

The next day, my mom picked me up and laid me down on the couch. Before she did that, I opened my eyes, smiled, and tried to ask her to promise me that she would be drug-free. But she'd just shush me. I could never fully get out what I wanted to say. So, I began to make picture books with words that had messages asking my mom to promise never to use drugs. I had no clue what being drug-free meant or what it looked like, but I wanted that for my mother. So, I'd make her these books on special occasions like Christmas, Mother's Day, and her birthday. For some reason, those books never lasted a year. I once made her a Christmas book and called it "My Christmas Gift to You." We still have that book to this day.

My mother finally went cold turkey and stopped doing drugs at the age of forty-nine—no rehab, no treatment. During the recovery period, her faith was tried and tested. By the second week, she experienced pain in her side, which, I would tell her, was a result of her lying down all day. During the third week, we had to rush her to the hospital because the part of her body just below her right breast was in a great deal of pain. We kept her in Sinai Samaritan Medical Center for three weeks. News broke out that she had the "big C-word." As a family, we knew nothing about that. My mom continuously thanked Jesus for helping her off the drugs; otherwise, she would have been unable to feel the pain from the cancer. It turned out that mom had small-cell lung cancer. She had to go through twelve rounds of chemo and have the upper left lobe of her lung cut out.

Given all of this, she did not go back to drugs. At the age of fifty-four, she got married. And yes, she still has her invisible friend, Jesus. I can say that He has been a great friend to my mother. Thank you, Jesus.

In 1991, during the same time my mom was addicted to drugs, my second-oldest sister, Neenee, suffered from sickle-cell anemia. So, when I wasn't tending to my mother, I'd be rubbing my sister, who would be in excruciating pain. Most nights, I'd rub her until it was time to go to school. She would be unable to go most times, but I'd go. Somehow, I wouldn't be tired either. I was happy just to see people pain-free or seemingly pain-free. I didn't care. All I knew was that I did not have to call Jesus, the imaginary friend, to my mother or sister. However, on some days, I felt very bad for my sister because I would be too tired to rub her. On such days, I would cry to myself, just like I'd do with my mother. But after crying, I would go on to rub her, after which she would fall asleep and wake up feeling like a normal child. That's all she wanted to be—a normal kid. It was hard for her to wrap her mind around the fact that she had a disease that even doctors did not know much about. This led to a change in her attitude. Being a very beautiful girl, people would have a hard time figuring out why she acted in such a poor, misbehaving manner. I think she was mad at mom's best friend, Jesus, for being a sickly child. Older folks would tell her that if she weren't so angry, she would not get sick. They had no idea about sickle-cell anemia. I don't think people understood or even cared about the fact that her poor behavior stemmed from her not knowing the unknown:

How long would she live?

Would she be able to get married?

Would she be able to have any children?

Would this get any worse?

As a young kid, watching Neenee deal with such immense pain hurt me on multiple levels for years. By the time she was a senior in high school, she was on her way to Taycheedah Correctional Institution.

People who go to prison tend to say this one thing a lot: it wasn't my fault. In this case, it was technically not her fault.

What happened was that I was smoking a blunt in my oldest sisters' apartment. Without my noticing, the police walked into the apartment. Long story short, they needed someone to take responsibility for the two bricks (pounds) of marijuana they found inside the house. I had no idea what to do in this situation; I felt helpless. So, I did what I knew best. I called on my mom's best friend, Jesus. Neenee ended up taking the marijuana case for me. On paper, she got three years. However, within a month, she got into some more trouble; her prosecutor had made false accusations against her. Needless to say, Neene did not follow her probation officer's guidelines as she was supposed to. This resulted in her getting a sentence of seven years.

At this point, I was already calling my mother's friend. By now, we all began to call on Jesus.

Neenee did only four years in prison, and the other three years were only on paper. During Neenee's four years in prison, I did not just lose my older sister—I lost my best friend. Don't get me wrong, I had plenty of people to speak to, but it didn't feel the same, and it wasn't the same. They didn't know who I was, and I would have to start my story from scratch. Neenee didn't need to be filled in with anything from scratch because she was there from the beginning. Even with my mom and other sister being there, it did not feel the same. Who could I speak to? Who could I have called on?

You guessed it right. I ended up getting my own imaginary/invisible friend, Jesus. The world says, "A friend in need is a friend indeed," but the Bible says, "Train up a child in the way he should go: and when he is old, he will not depart from it" (Proverbs 22:6 KJV).

My mom may not have taught us the traditional or even the normal way of knowing about Jesus. All I know Is that I have a great friend in His name: Jesus. "And call upon me in the day of trouble: I will deliver thee, and thou shalt glorify me" (Psalm 50:15 KJV).

If someone had you name three of your best friends, would Jesus be on the list? I would go on more about this, but my space in this book limits me. So, stay tuned.

Also, Neenee now has two children: a girl of eleven years and a boy of six years.

According to the Gospel of John, Jesus had a friend named Lazarus, whom he raised from the dead—because his sister called on Jesus. So, when people in your life fall sick, do you help them die, or do you call upon Jesus?

BIOGRAPHY

Jamie Stewart was born in St. Louis, MO, and raised in Milwaukee, WI, where she began to write at the tender age of seven. Jamie is a minister of Christ. She has helped a number of people come to Christ. She is also a world traveler, taking the good news with her as she explores this world one place at a time, spreading the gift of love. She currently holds an assistant teacher position for Milwaukee Public Schools and a ministerial position at Greater New Birth Church.

Connect with Jamie Stewart via https://linktr.ee/jamiess

CHAPTER 14

The Choice To Change

By Jessica Chingay

Have you ever hoped and dreamed for a different life? Ever wondered when all the things you've been working towards and dreaming of are actually going to happen? Ever feel stuck? Capped in your potential? I know I have. I came home from a prayer meeting this morning and saw the most incredible scene. My beautiful, wonderful, amazing three-year-old daughter sprawled out on my husband, both of them asleep in our bed. She had obviously woken up after I left, so she ended up on daddy's chest as he patted her back to sleep. How do I know this? Because I have seen it more than a few times. I can't even tell you how many photos I have of this exact scene! She likes to wake up early, and he likes to convince her that she is still tired. That way, he can sleep a little while longer! Ha! So funny! And there she was, still asleep on his bare chest, her curls in his face, both of them completely passed out, with our six-month-old sprawled out next to them. I am so grateful for these moments. They remind me of why I wanted to be a mom so desperately, why I wanted freedom in my life—the ability to have both time and money so that I could have choices. So that we could have choices. Like the choice we had to stay in bed a couple of hours longer because we wanted to and not worry about what time it was or whether we had to run off to work.

This lifestyle seemed so far away when I was growing up. I came from a background of poverty and abuse. My parents divorced when I was seven, and life seemed to spiral after that. I endured many years of emotional manipulation and extreme sexual abuse by multiple people. No matter which parent I lived with or what state I resided in, we moved every six months to a year, and it was always a new school, a new place to live, and new struggles to endure. We had family dynamics filled with rampant drug use and raw immorality in almost every sense of the word. This led to me carrying a strong atheistic belief system and fixed mindsets around how the world operated and how I could live. I was always a dreamer, though. I didn't really know how I would get it or if it was possible, but I believed, one day, I would steward millions. When I drove by large homes or nice cars, I somehow knew that I should have one of *those*. Not the broken-down two-bedroom trailer house we lived in that only had red-iron water coming out of its faucets, or the 98 Plymouth that I drove that had a hole in the trunk and a broken heater (this is a big deal when you live in North Idaho near Canada). At one point, we had about eighteen of us crammed in that two-bedroom trailer, and I got tired of my sisters partying at all hours of the night when I was trying to sleep, so I moved out on my own before turning fifteen. I was trying to put myself through high school while working two and three jobs at a time. Still out on my own, I couldn't make ends meet, so I began to sell drugs before I hit my sixteenth birthday. My morals were slipping. I was starting to compromise in ways I said I never would. That led me to have a two-year stint where I was essentially homeless. I would either live out of my car in the dead of winter (keep in mind I didn't have a working heater; one time, the sandwich I had made for lunch had frozen solid!) or I would be couch surfing with a friend or a guy I had hooked up with just to get a place to stay. It was a lonely road. I repeated the thing I hated: the only thing I had known. I spent too much time with the wrong crowd and eventually turned to partying, alcohol, sex, and drugs to cope. At one point, I moved into a huge house and filled it with roommates so that we could afford it and quickly turned it into the local party house. We put a stripper pole in the basement and had a tattoo artist in the living room. There wasn't a day that went by where that house was empty; it was always filled to the brim with people, and yet, I felt utterly alone. My relationships did not have any depth. I simply worked my three jobs and then partied and drank. My life was empty, and I was constantly drowning the fear and the pain I felt. I wanted a better future, but I was unable to see a pathway that would lead to it. My parents had done the best that they could with what they had and what they knew, but they had to work constantly to try to make ends meet, and that meant I had never really been parented, never guided in how to make decisions in life, how to manage my finances or make good relational choices. On top of that, I lacked the self-awareness it would take to truly grow as a person.

It was while I was living in this house that my whole life shifted. At the time, I worked three different jobs: a local taco shop franchise called Taco Time, Rosauers (a grocery store), and a caregiving program for people with disabilities. I would work for twenty-four to thirty-six hours straight with little to no sleep and then crash for half a day and start over. I never had any money, which led to days where I wouldn't eat. Sometimes, I would ration out a can of corn for two or even three days, never being honest or transparent with people around me about where I was really at.

Then, a gentleman came into my life who changed everything I ever thought I knew. He spoke about values, family, and marriage. He talked about living life on a budget and gaining financial independence so you could make the choices you wanted to make with your life. He was twenty-eight years old and about to walk away from a job forever when he showed me the business vehicle he had used to create those results. It radically transformed my life. He started mentoring me in how to make decisions, how to steward my finances, develop a faith, and start learning true principles of success. He was only ten years older than me, but he became a father, a brother, a business coach, a mentor, and a friend all at once. The business gave me so much hope—a chance for freedom, not just in my finances but in my life. The men he was running in life with spoke about concepts and principles I had never heard of before. Step by step, they taught me how to develop financial assets, set boundaries, change my mindsets, and change my life.

Then my life took another radical turn. I used a Ouji board and had a very supernatural encounter with God. That might turn you off or freak you out, but this is my story, and I can only share what happened to me. Now, I won't go into details, but that night I had the craziest dream. It felt entirely real. I was stepping off of a bus, and I could feel the freezing metal beneath my hands and the cold crisp air against my face. There was a firm woman in front of me, in full uniform, with the strictest facial expression I had ever seen. On her front pocket, it read, "U.S. Marine." I had joined the United States Marine Corps. As crazy as IT IS and as crazy as it sounds, believe it or not, the very next day, I got a call from a Marine Corps recruiter saying he had received my application and asking if I *still* wanted to join the Marine Corps.

I was flabbergasted. How did he get my application? I told him that I hadn't applied. He responded with, "I have your birth certificate right here on my desk. You are Jessica Reed, aren't you?" I was blown away. My birth certificate had gone missing a few months before. Who could have given it to them? I was about to protest, but recalling the dream I had the night before, I said YES.

Long story short, I *did* join the United States Marine Corps, and I met my husband in our specialty school right after boot camp. There is a whole other story in the middle of all that and a lot I went through, including breaking my hips and still finishing boot camp without anyone being aware of it. I don't have the time to tell you everything, but

I will say that those were the days that brought me the most radical self-awareness I had ever had. I was starting fresh and out of the muck and mire of my old life. I could hear my thoughts louder than ever before, and I realized that there were more options outside of the tiny mentality with which I was raised.

However, as with everything in life, the end of one story begins another. Though I had grown tremendously through boot camp and combat training, and I now knew what I wanted out of life, my husband, who was my boyfriend at the time, had his own journey to begin. Together, we were a bit toxic, to say the least. We had no idea how to love and value one another, and we fought *constantly*. We spent twelve to sixteen hours apart each day serving in the Marine Corps and had dug ourselves into a hole of about $75,000 worth of debt. We were back to partying and drinking all of the time and making a lot of immoral decisions that took us backward in many ways. I hit a wall. Is this why I had joined the Marine Corps? So that I could start back up my old lifestyle in a new place and a new way? No. I wanted MORE. I reached out to the people with whom I had previously been connected in business and started focusing on personal and financial growth again. They invited us to a Leadership conference with John Maxwell, but we didn't have the money to go. I said yes anyway. I scraped together whatever money I could find by selling a few things and by choosing not to pay my rent until we got back. I convinced my boyfriend to come and off we went. It was at *that* conference where we had a multi-millionaire named Bob speak some incredible life into us. As Mitchell was trying to ask him success questions and financial advice, he told Mitchell that if he wanted to be successful in anything in life, he would have to learn how to get committed and stay committed. He told him that to live with someone without being married was to "get the milk for free without buying the cow." You should have seen Mitchell's face; he looked like he had been hit by a Mack truck. Then, this guy said, "In Montana, we call that 'big

THE POWER OF LEADERSHIP

hat, no cattle, son." Mitchell didn't talk to me for the entire drive back home. He was so angry. He didn't want to be married until he was forty and we were only twenty-one, but you know what? A few weeks later, he proposed. And a few weeks after that, we fully surrendered our lives to Christ, got baptized, and got married. We made a commitment to each other and a commitment to grow and change. It was then that our whole life changed. We drew up our value system, made goals for ourselves, and started to live for a greater purpose than the daily grind. We sold our TV and started reading books together. We stopped hanging out with our beer-drinking buddies, and we sought after people who had the fruit in life that we wanted. We built friendships with people who were going where we wanted to go and started listening to audios and podcasts of people who had done what we needed to do.

Two years after that conversation with Bob, I resigned from what would be my very last job, and we moved to San Diego. What made all the difference in our life? The tiny choices to change, to be open-minded, to say yes to new things, to difficult things. We made one or two radical decisions to say yes and then backed it up with thousands of tiny baby steps—even when we were tired and doubting. We started to identify as the people we wanted to live like, which caused us to take actions towards our future, which produced the feelings, emotions, and results we wanted. We forced our decisions to lead us towards authentic relationships, which in turn transformed the way we thought and acted. I call this a Kairos moment: when something interrupts your normal pattern and starts to initiate a change in you. You may not notice the effects immediately, but if you take the risk and allow the moment to shift your direction, the compound effect will start to affect your mindset and awareness, and that cannot be undone. Maybe it's this book, a person you encountered, a conversation you had, or a job you took. But something at some point is going to interrupt the normal flow of your day-to-day lifestyle, habits, and thought patterns. *That* will be the start of your transformation! Let things interrupt you. Interruption is typically the beginning of the disruption of your average life. Take risks and step out on things that seem a little scary. Do something new for a change. Then listen to the way you think. Do your thoughts sound like those you want to emulate?

I believe the key to all success has always been and will always be relationships and daily habits. Most people call this your Association and lifestyle. The company you keep will determine the actions you take and the mindsets you break or live by. The key to breakthrough is not only the relationships you have but also the authentic communication within those authentic relationships. This is because when you can have someone with fruit in their life tell you the truth, you can start to become aware of what needs to change and start leading yourself or allowing them to lead you through the necessary shifts!

I also believe you have to take full, complete radical ownership of every little and big experience in your life. You must die to yourself and kill off victimhood. I love the book *Extreme Ownership* by Jocko Willink and Leif Babin. As long as you consider yourself a victim of your circumstance or find someone else to blame for anything that doesn't go right in your life, you will forever be stuck where you are. Keep this in mind as you navigate through this life: You are *never* finished. You will *never* arrive. You are *always* a work in progress and will never reach the pinnacle of success. You aren't meant to; you are meant to stay humble and continue to enjoy life's journey. Even after leaving my job and moving to sunny San Diego, there were seasons of frustration and dryness—seasons of feeling like no matter how hard we worked, we couldn't get traction in the goals we had. Do you want to know what the secret was every time we were stuck? The secret was that there was always something we *really* needed to learn—not to earn the next level in our life but to have the ability to steward it. We only learned these things, however, by remaining faithful and consistent in the tiny baby steps of change. Thomas Carlyle once said: "Adversity is sometimes hard upon a man, but for one man who can stand prosperity, there are a hundred that will stand adversity."[16] Meaning that for every 100 men that can handle adversity, only one can handle prosperity. Can you handle the weight of the responsibility of the things you are believing and praying for? Do you have it in you to lead the people, govern the business, and steward the finances you want? If you're not moving forward, there is more to learn. Work diligently and faithfully each day in the small one percent changes you can make to improve your mindsets, skill sets, relationships, and your health. Then you will be successful.

Why do you care about changing your life? I can tell you why I wanted to change mine. I want to be a woman who raises her own kids full-time and wins my children's respect and adoration for who I am as a mom while also having an incredible purpose and impact in the marketplace and the world. I want to change people's lives and set the captives free. I want to help people know and realize their full potential. I want to be an incredible wife and an example of marriage for others to follow. I want to give 100 times more money away than I used to live on. I want to give my parents the lifestyle they have ways dreamed of but were never able to make for themselves. I want to help others dream again and teach them how to make their dream a reality. I want to be an advocate for the Kingdom of God and raise Men and Women of Royalty.

What about you? What do you want? I can't tell you why you want to change your life. I can't tell you if you are actually sick and tired of being sick and tired. But I can tell you this: No one else is going to change your life for you. Only you can do that. And that will only

---

16   "Nearly All Men Can Stand Adversity, but If You Want to Test a Man's Character, Give Him Power," Quote Investigator, November 21, 2018, https:// quoteinvestigator.com/2016/04/14/adversity/.

happen by you choosing to change over and over again—by getting a little bit better each day, one baby-step at a time.

Get started. You can do this.

BIOGRAPHY

Jessica Chingay, a former United States Marine, has mentored and coached people in the direct sales industry since 2014. She left her traditional job in 2016 at the age of twenty-four and has gone on to own other top producing companies, including a large six-figure cleaning company. She also coaches other business owners and ministry leaders on successful living. She lives in sunny San Diego with her husband and two kids and spends her days writing, speaking, and mentoring others on how to access their callings and live out their destinies.

Connect with Jessica Chingay via https://linktr.ee/JessicaChingay

CHAPTER 15

From Innerstanding To Abundance

By LaDonia Frierson

If I told you every human being has the power to change their reality, to what extent would that be meaningful for you? Would you re-educate yourself to create more opportunities? Does the premise of working harder for what you desire come to mind? If you responded yes to these questions, allow me to share the story of how I figured this world out and learned to harness my power within to have an abundant life.

My childhood was nothing spectacular. It was quite typical for a little black girl growing up in Tampa, Florida, in the seventies and eighties. I dealt with the usual issues of being black during this time— being called a "nigger" or being egged. I recall our front door being spray-painted, "niggers leave," and my first friend in the neighborhood being called a "nigger-lover." I never allowed those actions to bring hatred into my heart. I had three brothers under me. I did my best to protect them from that kind of stuff—usually with my fists. I wasn't a bully, but the worst thing for anyone was for one of my brothers to tell me someone had bothered them. By the time I was fourteen, my reputation for beating up boys far preceded me. My brothers didn't have any known enemies. I was an average student at school. I was on the cheerleading team and enjoyed running track. I wasn't failing, but I wasn't an honors student either. Then, in junior high, we had the chance to gain work experience. I was able to leave school to develop some work skills at a local restaurant. Little did I know, this was not just going to be a job, but rather the start of my *Journey of Brokeness* (JOB).

At sixteen, my entire world suddenly changed. I was a junior in high school, a cheerleader…and pregnant with my first child. Her father stole my heart and my undies—silly me. My high school cheerleading status was short-lived. By 1986, I was seventeen and a teen parent of a beautiful baby girl, Ashley. The first lesson from my mother about motherhood was when she said, "You're going to need a JOB because I'm not taking care of your baby for you." My Journey of Brokeness continued. By graduation (in 1987), I aspired to be a nurse and have my own business. I wanted to have something I could leave to my child. I attempted junior college for approximately two weeks. I hated it! Nope, I did not go back to that. So, what else could I do? You guessed it: I was back on that Journey of Brokeness. I was eighteen and working at one of those pitstops on my journey when I met my first husband. We were married a year after meeting, and, at nineteen, I had my second beautiful baby girl, Amanda. Then, at twenty-one, I had twins—two bouncing baby boys, Ralph and Ronald. Their father was in the military, so we moved to Fort Campbell, Kentucky.

The Journey of Brokeness continued, but I held on to the dream of becoming a nurse and a business owner. I don't think my fingers and toes could count all the jobs I held or the businesses I tried to set up over the years. Tupperware, Herbalife, Kirby Vacuums, Cutco Cutlery, Avon, fast-food worker, telemarketer, home health aide, housekeeper, warehouse worker, security officer, cosmetologist…the list goes on. The home-based businesses were not as successful as I had hoped they would be. I didn't have the time to develop them because my need for income was so great that I had to keep working, or at least, that was my conditioning back then. Over the years, a common thread connected all those jobs: I really felt like I was an inmate in a workforce prison, with narcissistic or flat-out psychotic wardens in charge. Every new JOB was like a prison transfer with another warden.

During my twins' last year of high school, I decided to go to school myself as soon as they graduated. They graduated in 2010. I was in school immediately. I became a nurse in 2012. Being a nurse was a dream come true. My income doubled. Money was not an issue, but I was still an inmate. My most recent job as a nurse began my parole process from workforce prison. I loved what I was doing, but one thing bothered me: the pharmaceutical industry. I had seen many scenarios where older adults had to choose between meds and food or a bill that had to be paid. I thought about what people did before today's meds and technological advances. Mother Earth! *She* is flourishing with medicinals, from the bottom of the sea to the tops of mountains. Yet, herbalism seems to have been forgotten. I decided to study herbs. I took a Master Herbalist course to help myself and others.

However, studying herbs led me on an incredible transformational journey. In turn, this led me to discover the power of healing crystal energy. Learning about all the beautiful crystals and their capabilities was intriguing. I was captivated by this "healing energy." From there, I discovered even more about healing energy, more specifically, Reiki. I learned about symbols and hand gestures to harness healing energies. I became a Level 4 Practitioner and Master Teacher. I learned the power of mindfulness when channeling and meditating. And just when I thought it couldn't get any more amazing, I discovered an author whose teachings were the most profound I had ever come across because they resonated with my feelings about certain things found in the Bible. Reading these books left me excited, and I found myself saying, "I knew it!" often. This was my introduction to the Universal Laws and the Law of Attraction (LOA).

I understood the LOA: Think it, Believe it, See it, Feel it! Intentions and affirmations flowed. I started manifesting things and situations like homeownership, buying a car on my terms, and having my own business tailored to my desires. Yet, I knew there must be more! It was like pieces were missing from the puzzle. Intuitively, I hungered for more knowledge. I discovered videos that echoed the teachings of the author I mentioned earlier, but there was something different. I was so drawn that I explored as far as I could to find more about the content in the videos. I learned that the teachings were based on communication with a higher intelligence. Boldly and with confidence, I call it SOURCE ENERGY, but there are many names for it: God, The One, Allah, Jehovah, and many more. And they all have one thing in common: They all represent the Highest Truth, from which all things come into existence. As I listened to more of these teachings, things began to fall in place. My understanding became MY INNERSTANDING. I came to understand that everything I *ever* wanted started *inside me*. This was my *AWAKENING*!

Innerstanding has four basic branches. As you learn more, the branches grow like a tree, forking and growing. Your FAITH is the fertilizer!

- You must KNOW and define Source Energy.
- You must understand YOUR RELATIONSHIP with Source Energy.
- You must understand YOUR POWER within as it relates to Source Energy.
- You must know how to COMMUNICATE YOUR DESIRES to Source Energy for a Life of Abundance.

That was the point when my outlook on life and my perspective forever changed. The realization of who I AM and what I AM capable of doing floored me. Thinking of the struggles I could have missed out on made me a little salty.

The Innerstanding

Source Energy is pure, positive, flowing energy in all of us. We are sons and daughters of Source Energy. Gods and Goddesses, no different than Jesus, except Jesus had this "Innerstanding" from birth. He was always awake. It is why he was set apart and marked for greatness. We have the power to give form to thought, as does Source Energy. Our thoughts, words, and feelings vibrate at their own frequency. Source Energy, and nothing else, delivers these vibrations (our VIBRATIONAL FEELINGS).

Grasping this takes an insurmountable amount of FAITH. It requires deliberate thought processes. The same way planning an event and lining up every detail is how you must plan your desires and mentally line up every detail. I lived all my life not realizing I could change my thought process and have all I desired.

Sadly, most people do the same. As babies, we are taught things by our parents, grandparents, and other family members. Then, we're taught by teachers who teach us from books that someone else wrote. Then, there's society, with its worldly influences. Our decisions and thoughts are solely based on our life experiences. Not knowing our abilities, we succumb to our surroundings and life as it appears before us. We do this reflexively, like a knee-jerk reaction, because it's all we have known. Our ancestors may have attempted to tell us differently, with writings on walls, but what they had to say has been translated in so many different degrees that the very message about the true beings we are has been misconstrued or lost.

Not once have we (or do we) stop reacting and decide, at any moment, that we are going to do something else besides react. We have been led to believe we must play with the hand we are dealt with and live life. Many manage to do just that because they pursue education or some type of career. Those choices are reactions based on their surroundings. Most were taught to go to college for a better education to get that better career. Those choices or decisions are simple reactions to what they were taught.

We are taught this from day one and, hence, believe that working hard and sometimes struggling will bring us all we desire. But think about it: Source Energy created us from thought, and Source Energy is within us. Therefore, it is reasonable that we should be able to create a perfect, abundant life. So, is ignorance really bliss, as they say, or not?

Because of my personal experiences with abundance, I'm so driven to share. The moment you gain Innerstanding will be the moment a gateway opens, and ABUNDANCE WILL FLOW! Not just specific desires but unexpected ones, too! Now, I know this may be a lot to take in. It was for me! It's just the tip of the iceberg. So, let me share how I started down this abundant path and what I still do to this day. I choose to believe things are *always* working for ME, without question and doubt! I choose this *deliberately* and *faithfully*. I express my gratitude for everything I have experienced! I AM forever grateful, and who wouldn't be?! Imagine a world where things *always* work out for you, even when they might appear not to! You can't help but feel good about that and be grateful!

Source Energy wants everyone to be happy and live a life of prosperity and abundance. Go beyond your human experience. Take the time to discover your Innerstanding and learn to live the *abundant life* we all so richly deserve.

BIOGRAPHY

LaDonia Frierson is an author, lightworker, life coach, and entrepreneur. She's a member of the International Association of Therapists (IAOTH), with certifications and practitioner status in Reiki Levels 1–4, Crystal Healing, and Chakra Healing. She is a gateway to the angelic realm through Angel Tarot Readings and Angel Light Hypnosis. Helping others discover their *Innerbeing* for a life of abundance brands her coaching and charges her entrepreneurial spirit. Her goals far exceed financial gain. She takes pride in helping others break out of the "workforce prison" to find their path of abundance. Unwavering faith in Source Energy's provision is her success catalyst.

Connect with LaDonia Frierson via https://llcsolutions.pro/Contact-Doni/

CHAPTER 16

Searching For The Smartest Way To Make A Good Life

By Morten Andersen

I had been waiting for the message. I had looked forward to this day for a year. I looked at the CEO and said, "Thank you," and hurried back to my office. Sat down, closed my eyes, and started to cry.

Why did I feel like that? After all, it's what I wanted. Why am I so sad? Why do I feel this overwhelming sense of loss?

It was my life, my top priority, and my identity—I had spent all my time and energy on it for eight years. And now, it's over. I packed a few things and left the office. None of my eighty-five employees knew yet. It was the last time I saw most of them.

At home, I told my wife what had happened. She warmly hugged and congratulated me. That's when I first noticed the feeling of freedom. It was barely noticeable in the sea of sadness, confusion, and fear, but it was there.

Fourteen years earlier, when graduating from engineering school, I started my first job as a software and hardware developer in a husband-and-wife company. Being their first employee, it was the closest to being an entrepreneur myself. As the company grew, I engaged in all kinds of work: project management, sales, customer support, delivering training courses, and production, in addition to my main job developing software and hardware. What a great way to learn!

This was also when I was first introduced to network marketing. I was blown away by the concept, and we started out as part-time network marketers. We never made it big in that company, but we learned a lot about sales and entrepreneurship.

I remained in my first job for five years. Being an employee, without a doubt, had its benefits: decent salary, interesting job, good colleagues, great business travels, and flexible working hours. There was nothing to complain about. Most of my colleagues from my previous jobs are still employees. For them, it's clearly the right thing.

For me, it was not. I wanted to create my future, not working for someone else. In 1991, I was ready. I knew that starting my own company was going to be hard work. It would be tough to live without a salary for weeks, or maybe months. I was totally fine with it!

I founded the company together with two friends, and our first office was the guest bedroom in my home. We developed advanced software for the telecom industry, obtained our first few customers, and six months later, we were able to move into a real office.

The first two years, we paid ourselves very little, often nothing, so we could employ more people, move to a bigger office, and grow. I worked at least eighty hours a week, and it was fun. It's incredible what is possible when running on pure ambition, enthusiasm, and the joy of creating something from nothing!

For me, it was all about freedom. My definition of freedom was not to avoid work; it was to create, to not have a boss telling me what I can and cannot do, and of course, to have the possibility of a very good income, much more than any regular job would ever pay.

But the freedom came with a price, and after three years, we had to give up our plan to grow without investors. Growth costs money, lots of money. Developing more products, increasing marketing activities, and selling more meant that we needed even bigger offices, more equipment, more inventory, and more employees.

With investors on board, we continued the growth. With eighty-five employees, we developed and sold expensive solutions to big telecom operators in twenty-five countries. When we were finally ready to enter the US market, we decided to partner with a company from Virginia. They needed what we had, and they ended up buying the company.

Moneywise, it was great. I got well paid for my share of the company. I had no problem signing for the one condition they had: the three founders would have to stay in the company for three years.

It turned out to be a big problem. After six years of hard work, with responsibility for numerous employees and customers, taking risks, and having had very little time off, I was tired. The enthusiasm I used to have was gone. The feeling of freedom I initially had was also gone. I had gone from being an enthusiastic, creative, free entrepreneur to a burnt-out employee.

Have you ever experienced a real burn-out? I mean, not temporarily being exhausted and needing a vacation, but being entirely stripped of energy and not finding any joy or enthusiasm for the things you do anymore. Everything becomes hard. You just want to quit, escape, sleep, and not talk to anyone.

I did my best to do a decent job as CTO of the company. I became pretty good at hiding what I truly felt and disciplining myself to do what I needed to do. And, of course, it only got worse. One day I just had to admit that this was it; I could not take it anymore. I told the CEO and asked the board to release me from the contract. It took over a year before they did.

Free. Finally. Burnt-out, but free. It took me a week to recover from the worst sadness and feeling of disappointment in myself. At the end of the week, the potential of a fresh start got more and more exciting, but I still did not know what I wanted, only what I did not want.

Should I go back to being a regular employee? In a way, it was tempting—a fixed salary every month, normal working hours, and no responsibility for the company. If something happened, I could just find myself another job. With my experience, I could have found a great, well-paying job.

Should I start a new company? If so, what would I do? What kind of business? And most importantly, how would I avoid what put me in this situation?

My friends told me to get a regular job. After all, that's what *they* did. The more I thought about having a job, the clearer it became. I'm an entrepreneur. I have tasted the feeling of freedom, and I want it again.

So, I decided to give the dream another chance, and this time it should be different. I decided that no matter what kind of business I started, it had to fulfill my no-negotiable requirements:

1. No employees, no expensive offices, or other big overhead costs

2. No external investors, requiring very little capital for growth

3. Very high-income potential

4. No opening hours or fixed working hours

5. Interesting work where I can express myself, use my creativity, learn, and grow

6. Must be meaningful to me and to my clients/customers; something of which I will be proud

I don't mind working hard, as long as I do it with enthusiasm and freedom. Then it's not really work; it's a lifestyle of contribution, growth, and expression.

I believe what we get is what we focus on. I was so obsessed with finding the right business idea that I know what happened next was no coincidence. I saw an ad in *Entrepreneur Magazine* for a "Small Business Expo" in Dallas. Living in Norway, Dallas was far away, but I felt I just had to go there. That's where I met the person that re-introduced me to network marketing.

I did have years of experience from network marketing as a side business, more like a hobby, but I had not considered it as a "real" business before. Looking at my list of requirements and what a serious network marketing business in a good company would be like, I understood that this probably was exactly what I had been looking for.

We went all in. We started with the clear intention and goal of going *to the top* of our chosen company. This was not going to be a "try and see" thing like we had treated our previous network marketing side business.

We decided to work as professionals from day one. After many years as an employee and running my own company, I had no problems treating this as a professional business the same way. One of my goals was time-freedom with no fixed working hours. But that does not mean *no* working hours; it means deciding your own working hours.

I knew that going to the top requires that we learn from those already at the top, from the best. It's like when I decided to become an engineer, I did not learn to become a professional software and hardware developer from a random friend. I did not think that I was better than my teachers at engineering school. Of course not. I learned from the best, and gradually became a great engineer.

I applied the same principle in my network marketing business. I listened to my sponsor and mentors, took their advice, did the activities, and it worked.

I remember they told me there will be challenges like in any other business, and to reach the top, you must accept that challenges are a part of the business, and life. Going to the top, building a great business means working through the challenges and leveraging them to learn, grow and become stronger. Not understanding this is why most people in network marketing fail and ultimately quit.

Treating the business as a business paid off, and we reached the company's top position in less than four years. With that came several recognitions such as "Distributor of the Year" more than once, becoming members of the millionaire's club, and other cool perks.

But most importantly, I had created a business that fulfilled everything on my list, i.e., all my non-negotiables! I got the life I wanted, a life of freedom. I could work from home and be home when the kids came back from school. I could go on a three-week vacation whenever I wanted, without having to ask for time off.

The feeling of doing something important was also an essential factor; changing the lives of thousands for the better by helping others start their own businesses and experience the amazing benefits of the products!

The contrast to the life I had in my previous business and as an employee was huge!

It was about thirty-five years ago I started my first network marketing side business, and I have been a full-time network marketer for over twenty years now. I have also funded and been involved in a few new "traditional" companies over those years, all made possible by the residual income and time freedom I got from network marketing.

To me, network marketing has paved the way to business-freedom, life-freedom, and living up to my fullest potential. I'm an entrepreneur by heart; I like to create and build businesses. And the great thing about network marketing is that the building and growing never stops, unless you want it to. You can take it as far as you like; there are no upper limits.

The potential in network marketing is so immense that I decided to stop all activities with my other businesses a few years ago. Network marketing is all about helping others become the best they can be, regardless of the company they are associated with. It's a profession of service to others, making a change in the world, and creating more freedom.

Having been an employee and an employer, having had network marketing as a side business and a main business, I know what's right for me. I know I can help anyone who wants a fulfilling life and freedom to succeed. Network marketing is truly the best and the most fair business model for this century.

BIOGRAPHY

Morten Andersen is a passionate entrepreneur and business coach. He started his career as an employee, developing software and hardware. He has been an employer of the three technology companies which he started. Morten has also built large, international businesses as a network marketer. With thirty-five years of extensive experience from all sides of business life, this book is vital for anyone that considers starting a business and dreams of a better life. Morten has previously written two books about business. He's an experienced speaker and has been speaking at several business conferences in Europe, the USA, and China. And with his long experience as a successful network marketer, he is a sought-after trainer and mentor. He loves traveling, experiencing new countries, cultures, and food.

Contact Morten Andersen via http://www.mortenandersen.info

CHAPTER 17

The Power Of Self-Confidence

By Okiemute Ojeh

As I was drifting into slumber, I suddenly felt the wave of cold chills running down my spine. My heart started pounding. It was so fast and loud it felt like it was going to drop out of my chest. I attempted to sit up. I could not. I resorted to crawling out of my bed to the floor (thankfully, it was a low frame). I began to gasp for air because my throat became too narrow to let air in, and I shivered in fear. I could not move my body. I tried to scream for help—no sound could escape. Though my mobile phone was well within reach, I could not lift my arms to get it. My mind raced! My heart kept pounding. I panicked, scared to my bones that I would not make it through the night.

My five-year-old son was peacefully asleep, enjoying the night and totally oblivious to the ongoing drama. I looked at him and shook my head. My heart sank in despair: hot, sad tears rolled down my face. What would become of him? How would he take it? How would he cope? Those thoughts kept plaguing my mind as I lay helplessly on the floor in my room in Southeast London. As I thought about these questions in my mind, I managed to whisper a word of prayer. How did I get here? What happened to my amazing, fun-filled, sweet life? How did everything suddenly fall apart? Where did I go wrong? What did I do to deserve all the bitter pills life shoved down my throat? What could I have done differently? I asked myself these questions a zillion times!

I was not born with a silver spoon. However, my doting parents pampered and raised us with the best things in life—love, joy, and discipline. That was the lens through which I saw life!

After bagging a bachelor's degree in microbiology, I tied the knot with my best friend. Do you know that feeling of being with someone who gets you and you get them in return? That was Michael. We had lots of fun times together. Sixteen months after our wedding, we welcomed our cute baby. Our families were beside themselves with joy! Could life be any better? We were reveling in the loving arms of our families and friends.

Two months before the fifth anniversary of our wedding, I became pregnant with our second child. Imagine our joy! It was short-lived. Just a couple of days into the pregnancy, we realized it was going to be a turbulent ride—a threatened miscarriage had set in. The medical personnel worked hard to save the pregnancy. I was very weak, unable to do anything.

Fortunately, I had my family next door. They took me in and practically did everything for me. Exactly two weeks and four days to our fifth wedding anniversary, Michael got back home from work and complained of a headache. That was strange and got me slightly worried. He was not one to experience headaches. The following morning, he complained of some discomfort in his stomach and that he regurgitated the previous night. That made me scared. My dad called to check on us, and I told him things were not looking good. When I mentioned Michael's situation, he immediately made arrangements for my mom to join us.

How was I supposed to know that that was a prelude to a new phase of my life?

As my health gradually began stabilizing, Michael's deteriorated. The next thing I knew, he was in the emergency unit of the biggest hospital in the city where we lived. The results of the series of laboratory tests he took did not look good. On a daily basis, I'd go to the hospital for my pre-natal care (because of the threatened miscarriage), then go to the facility where my husband was admitted. My cousin was my chauffeur; he drove me everywhere I needed to go. In the midst of this turmoil, I wrote my final exam for the postgraduate course I was taking. How I was able to write that exam amid the chaos beats me to date. Two days before our fifth anniversary, my husband was moved to the Intensive Care Unit (ICU). Our bosom buddy came to the hospital the following day and immediately broke down in tears when he saw Michael in the ICU.

On Thursday, November 29, 2007, our fifth wedding anniversary, I woke up early, got ready, and requested to be taken to the hospital. I wanted to spend as much time as possible with Michael. I wanted to talk to him, remind him of all our dreams and the fun things we had planned to do together. I wanted to get him a special card. My big brother was home. As I was asking him why he did not go to work, my phone rang. He snatched it and took the call…Michael was gone! That morning—the same day we clocked five years of marriage. I froze. Time stopped. My hands and legs trembled. I asked for my phone and called our friends. Some of them were at the hospital. I desperately waited to hear that it was a mistake. No, it was true.

How did I get here? Widowed at thirty-one with a three-year-old son, two months pregnant, and absolutely no idea of how to proceed from there. It was the darkest day of my life. How does one go from so happy to utterly miserable?

All my family members solidly rallied around and supported me in the days, weeks, months, and years that followed. My friends did the same. Despite the amazing support, I would go to bed at night, wondering why it had to be on *that day*! Why did our five years journey begin and end on the same day? Why did he leave?

Seven months after Michael's exit, still in the quagmire of anxious and depressing thoughts, I gave birth to my second son. The process was the most horrendous experience of my life! I actually felt my life slipping away—it was a narrow escape. I was sore all over. However, I anticipated meeting my baby. I waited and looked longingly at the door each time it opened, expecting to see him. When the phone rang, my mom and big sister-in-law would hurriedly walk out of the room to receive the call and speak in hushed voices. My mind started racing. Something was definitely not right here. My big brother came, spoke consolingly to me, and left after a while. Still no baby. Different family members called and spoke to me in circles. Then, I knew for sure that the baby did not make it out alive. The following day, I was taken home. I told my mom and big sister-in-law that I knew the baby was dead. It was glaring from all the activities of the previous night. Within seven months, I lost and buried two people, Michael, my best friend and husband, and my unnamed second son. A part of me was gone. My heart sank; the burden was too much for me to bear. I was losing my mind.

With the support of my family, I relocated from Nigeria to England. That was where I experienced the panic attacks described at the beginning of the story. I returned to Nigeria a couple of years later.

I started rebuilding my business, which collapsed some months after my husband's death. A short while after that, I got an excellent, well-paying job. The income from both sources was great, so I commenced developing the property we (Michael and I) had purchased. Suddenly the oil crisis hit the world. That resulted in many employees losing their jobs. Unfortunately, I made the list. June 30, 2015, I was retrenched. Another blow below the belt!

A year later, a regulatory organization knocked down the property I was developing. All the necessary documentation for the land had been completed before construction commenced. What went wrong? All the money poured into that property went down the drain. Yet another blow below the belt!

My life was punctuated with difficult challenges. I was really angry with life. Why did I always have to have my back against the wall? I lost my inner joy and sleep. On so many nights, I would watch every hour go by. There were several occasions when I wanted to throw in the towel. Do you know the feeling of wanting to get some fresh air?

A little voice kept holding me back.

That voice came from an unexpected event that happened years back in my final year of high school. A teacher in the school discovered that a student had paid a bribe to swap my exam scripts. The exam board was alerted, and they set up a committee to investigate the report. The committee invited everyone involved to an investigation session. What broke my heart most was the fact that the student who "bought" my exam scripts was my close friend. "Why?" Just when I thought I heard everything, the committee presented their findings: more than one student was involved. I was dumbfounded! On our way back home, my teacher (who discovered the fraud) told me something and implored me to always remember it. He said I have great potentials, and that incident was just an obstacle to distract me from focusing on the great things ahead. He looked at me sternly and said: "Whatever obstacle you meet in your journey, see it as a distraction."

Each time I experienced a challenge, I literally went numb. I lost my grit. I complained and moaned about my troubles. That, in turn, led to the loss of my inner strength and motivation to take action. That was it—*distraction*! It led to inactions.

Pressure from the barrage of challenges led to some messy situations because of not-well-thought-out decisions. However, I never forgot my teacher's remarks. Achieving my full potentials depended on my ability to rise above "distractions" that interjected my journey.

I worked hard on developing grit, which led to building my self-confidence.

Self-confidence has helped me to see the challenges from the right perspective—as distractions aimed at making me take my eyes off the target. So, I keep my targets (my goals) constantly in front of me. When I remember that succumbing to the challenge would mean forfeiting my goals, I get energized to take action one more time. Simple, right? No. Possible? Absolutely!

Henry Ford said: "Obstacles are those frightful things that you see when you take your eyes off your goal."[17] Could he be any further from the truth?

Self-confidence is a key ingredient in overcoming challenges.

Psychology Dictionary Online defines self-confidence as an individual's trust in his or her own abilities, capacities, and judgments, or belief that he or she can successfully face day-to-day challenges and demands.[18]

Overcoming challenges is more the state of one's mind than any external factor. Why is it that when two people experience the same problem, one overcomes it while the other does not? It is simply a matter of mindset. The first has an excellent dose of self-confidence; the latter does not.

If you are self-confident, the little voice in your head tells you, "It is possible." This produces positive energy flow, which results in action.

---

17 "Henry Ford Quotes," BrainyQuote (Xplore), accessed December 10, 2021, https://www.brainyquote.com/quotes/henry_ford_101486.

18 "APA Dictionary of Psychology," American Psychological Association (American Psychological Association), accessed December 10, 2021, https://dictionary.apa.org/self-confidence.

One of my mantras is:

> *"Whether you think you can, or you think you can't—you're right."*[19]
>
> *—Henry Ford*

Every challenge you overcome increases your level of self-confidence. If this is lacking, it is almost impossible to overcome your challenges, even with a powerful support system. You will self-sabotage because you do not have confidence in yourself. When they say you can do it, the negative voice in you will say, "It is not possible."

Self-confidence helped me flourish under the support of my entire family. I saw possibilities and took action! Fourteen years after Michael, I have completed two postgraduate courses, rebuilt my business twice, and relocated myself and my son to my dream country, just to mention a few milestones.

This is my gift to you: "The ability to overcome any challenge is in *you.* Grow your grit, build your self-confidence and crush your goals!"

BIOGRAPHY

Okiemute Ojeh is the CEO of Spicy Ite Training Systems. A professional in environmental conservation and occupational health and safety, Okiemute spent the last decade working with different organizations. These presented her the opportunity to observe how an untold number of talents go down the drain due to a lack of self-confidence. For over four years, Okiemute has been mentoring people with natural and acquired diffidence. She provides her service in person and through online social media platforms. Her great leadership, spiced with genuine concern for people, has helped many find their inner motivation to dream again.

---

19   "A Quote by Henry Ford," Goodreads (Goodreads), accessed December 10, 2021, https://www.goodreads.com/quotes/978-whether-you-think-you-can-or-you-think-you-can-t--you-re.

Inspiring people to believe in themselves is a continuous burning desire in her. "Spicy Ite," as Okiemute is fondly called, lives in the Queen City of Canada with her family. She loves the smell of books, is passionate about rugged toys and reggae, and is great at connecting with people.

Connect with Okiemute Ojeh via https://linktr.ee/SpicyIte

CHAPTER 18

Thrive In Adversity

By Patrice Maurer

Thriving is an attitude, one like Nietzsche wrote about. What does not kill you makes you stronger.[20]

But if you were my friend and needed my advice to survive a life of tragedy that brought pain and suffering, this is NOT what you would want to hear. In fact, if I were to tell you "Never give up" and "Whatever you must face, it will be worth it," you would dismiss me from your home and possibly your life.

And you would be right to do so.

So, I will not give you hollow words or some dead philosopher's quote. Instead, may I share with you how I overcame one adversity after another and decided not just to learn to survive but rather thrive in real-life adversity?

As a little boy, I just knew I had a great destiny. That I would somehow receive an important mission in life. I simply could not have imagined what I would have to face to overcome challenges along the way.

---

20 "Friedrich Nietzsche Quotes," BrainyQuote (Xplore), accessed March 30, 2021, https://www.brainyquote.com/quotes/friedrich_nietzsche_101616.

My mother and father were ordinary hard-working people. I came to understand that I arrived a little too soon. My mother stayed at home to educate my sister and me. My sister came along three years after I did, followed by my brother four years later. My mother only went back to work when my brother was fourteen years old.

My father worked hard, worked overtime, built our house, made a career in the factory where he worked, and climbed the social ladder until his retirement. He is still enjoying his retirement today at over seventy-nine years of age. His example is my model of righteousness, rigor, and perseverance.

Life was grand, and our family was loving. We grew happily despite minor sibling disputes.

When I began nursery school, I spoke only the Alsatian dialect. Alsace is a region in eastern France, along the German border, where the dialect was still prevalent in the 1960s and 1970s. It is a dialect close to German (75% German, 25% French). But despite pressure from the French government after the Second World War, with the return of Alsace to France, they could not manage to make it disappear. So, by my time in elementary school, I was fluent in French.

My elementary teacher oddly noted on my report card that I was a dreamer. I remember the event very well because she scolded me with the same comment so often. It may have been this dreaming that attracted attention from bullies who would routinely beat me up. I never understood why. I just felt betrayed!

The bullying continued throughout secondary school, and I was not a fighter at all. So, I just endured the violence. Eventually, I became unstable, and my grades started to plummet. And even though math was my favorite subject in primary school, I lost interest in it, leading my father to scold me that I didn't work enough, that I dreamed too much, and that I played too much. He would make me feel inadequate by comparing me to children who had better grades and to my cousin.

But it was true. My escape from life was my playtime. So, I played in secret.

This conflict continued. My father pushed me into math. But I hated it. What I loved was foreign to him. My passions included history, collecting rare coins, and I simply loved to read, devouring book after book.

And yes, I still dreamed a lot, despite all the scolding.

To escape, I searched for a solution. I got a job during college. There were no alternatives, and I had applied to the professional hotel school. If I had not been accepted there, there would have been no choice other than an apprenticeship.

For me, it was obvious; I would be accepted into hotel school. But my parents, always so scared and indecisive, passed their doubts and fears onto me. Looking back, I realize that generation functioned entirely from a place of self-doubt: a prison made of self-induced fear.

From this place, I learned to struggle with self-doubt. Becoming fragile from the constant bullying, I grew into a victim. The harassment reached its peak with bullies knocking me off my bike. Scratched and bewildered, I stood up. I faced the pack of laughing hyenas without so much as a flinch. On my way home, I wondered: is this my future?

Imagine my relief when I graduated from secondary. I felt it was a fresh start, one where bullies no longer existed. But this "beginning" would last for the next forty-five years! I was an insecure seventeen-year-old! I did not feel that I was moving towards my dream of becoming an important and recognized person. I wasn't popular, I didn't have the drive, and I hadn't chosen the easiest path. It was 1982: my first year at the hotel school.

After several false starts in the hospitality industry, I found a job in Germany at a gastronomic restaurant in Freiburg, Breisgau. A young French chef gave me my start. But from the beginning, I was frustrated that I was preparing delicacies for people who were enjoying life on the other side of the wall, whereas I was stuck in that kitchen.

I was determined to make a considerable change, so I joined the army! For the first eighteen months, I served as the bartender in the NCO's mess. But very quickly, I understood that this also was not what I was looking for.

After the army, I went to work in Basel, Switzerland, but returned to France, where I was hired at the restaurant for Peugeot's car factory executives in Mulhouse. There, I rebelled—the same scenario. I realized that I was *not* made to work in those environments. The same scenario would systematically repeat itself. My history of switching from one restaurant to another only displaced the problem from one place to the next. It was a carousel: same problem, different city.

I noticed the salespeople who sold products to the chefs I worked with. I dreamed of changing my life, and becoming a salesman seemed intriguing. So, after I applied, I was interviewed by a psychologist, who told me that I was unfit for the job.

I felt disappointment, but no sense of resignation!

Shortly afterwards, I discovered network marketing. I had my first clients and several partners. And I attended my first seminar in Paris. It was there that I realized that my life was going to change. Cooking in a kitchen for the rest of my life was over as of 1989. But this first experience shortly expired.

An associate suggested I complete a personality test. One thing led to another, and I began to delve into Scientology. This was something I had never heard of before, and I soon found myself in Copenhagen. The subject seemed interesting, discussing personal development and helping people to become free, rising through their programs. And, once again, I learned a lot.

This is where my character began to really assert itself because I drew from it what seemed most valuable to me, without entirely adhering to the Scientology philosophy. The negative aspects were that we worked endless hours with almost no freedom, very poor compensation, and total control. Yet, I persisted for over two years. I had become an essential element. I not only learned to use the computer tool, distributing all intranet messaging in the company, but I ended up managing their kitchen. And that is where I finally became autonomous in the kitchen and gained self-confidence!

I returned to France in 1993 and quickly found a job in direct sales for an internationally renowned German company. After four years, I performed well and became the agency's top salesman several times. I spearheaded an agency in Rennes, where I rose to sales coordinator in 1995, and one in Vannes. It was there that I met the woman who was to become my wife. We married in 1999, and my daughter was born soon after that.

With my acquired experience in sales, I believed the psychologist who had told me just a few years earlier that I was not made for sales. In 1997, I fulfilled a dream of mine—reconciling sales and cooking—by joining a regional company that sold frozen food products to professionals in the food trade! It was a great experience. I exploded the scores, increasing sales by 33% in May 1998.

But what was supposed to be a madly exciting step quickly turned into a nightmare. The new manager took advantage of a drop in sales to trick me into signing an amendment to the employment contract. I believed I would earn more commissions, but the opposite happened.

In the midst of all this, during an annual visit to the occupational physician, the doctor advised me to get vaccinated against hepatitis B on the pretext that I was in regular contact with food products. This was during a vaccination campaign. After the second injection, I woke to realize that I could no longer walk. I was diagnosed with multiple sclerosis.

At that time, I was fortunate to meet an "enlightened" doctor who made me read a few books and made me aware of several things. I do not know if it was the vaccine that caused it or the combination with the stress I was experiencing at the time. It still took a month to recover.

For me, it was unthinkable that this disease would take over. I had just started a career. I had found a path that I liked, and I was doing very well. I was winning markets! This company convinced me to return to Alsace to develop the region, but these were more promises that failed to materialize.

I chose food packaging. But my illness was manifesting itself more and more slyly, with loss of sensitivity, my balance becoming fragile, and my gait becoming more and more difficult.

Though not the best company, I remained loyal for seven years because I was beginning to lack the self-confidence to change and start again elsewhere. My deteriorating health only increased my worries. At one point, the stress of the poor atmosphere became too unbearable. So, I made a change one last time. This new company promised higher pay, but after fifteen months. But my body said "Stop!"

The end of my commercial career! I could no longer cope with the long commute and all the walking. I had a total of three crises in 2009.

But I refused to give up! I would not accept defeat! I still had my dream. I just knew something would come up.

I tried banking, but that was not it either. I felt in my soul that I deserved something else. And I believed that no employer deserved me. I had given too much and suffered too many betrayals and psychological bullying! I wanted to live and be free, to bring my light to the world. And I realized how much I'd learned during all these years through all the meetings and after years of research.

Despite my refusal to give up on my dream, the last crisis confined me to a wheelchair in 2014. Fatigue became increasingly challenging to manage. Financially, it was difficult. I ended up on a disability pension which dropped my income by half.

Luckily, my wife had her salary. But in 1995, she was found to have a brain tumor. An emergency operation followed with severe after-effects. She was never able to recover and fully return to work. She had also become disabled.

Fate continued to challenge us! The relentless setbacks felt extremely difficult. I wondered what the universe was trying to reveal to me. I recovered, but I must admit that doubt haunted me night and day. It was difficult to retain positive thoughts when so much had gone wrong.

I continued searching. After testing several products from various MLM companies, I found a technology that influences the cells. My extreme fatigue ended, after overwhelming me for several years with ever-increasing intensity, in no more than two weeks. Amazingly, more improvements followed. And, finally, a trustworthy company, with a high level of ethics and a genuine philosophy.

The last three years have shown continual improvement, economically and health-wise. My illness seems to have stopped progressing and I have resumed a full-time professional career from home.

For once in my life, I am enthusiastic about the future and extremely grateful for the progress I've made with associates and clients.

My journey has been painful and difficult: betrayals, setbacks, roadblocks, injustices, and unfairness at a level that made me want to just give up and quit on many, many nights. But taking on each obstacle, I discovered that I had choices: surrender, settle, make excuses, quit, or just give up.

But in those moments, I can tell you, I never gave up! I believed within the depth of my soul that whatever I had to face would somehow be worth it! And I determined that what did not kill me only made me stronger!

So, I'm not here to be exiled from your life by spouting hollow phrases and philosophy devoid of any meaning. In fact, that important mission I dreamed of was to be part of your life—right here, right now. You see, I have achieved the dream I made as that little boy so many years ago that *decided to believe in his great destiny*—that I would somehow get chosen to make a difference in your life. No, I could not have imagined the things I had to face to overcome the difficulties along the way. But I'm here, in this moment, to inspire you never to give up, to endure anything because the test is worth it, and that the challenges from life that do not kill you only make you stronger!

BIOGRAPHY

Patrice Maurer knew from an early age that he would have an extraordinary destiny. Thanks to his solidly anchored belief, he has been able to persevere through every obstacle. It began with childhood bullies and continued through his professional career. The rollercoaster ended the moment he decided to change! The revelation that his life failed to correspond to what he had dreamed of achieving in life fuelled this decision. It took endless failures and soul-wrenching endurance to discover what he'd imagined in his mind. Today, after coming full circle back to his city of birth, Patrice lives his dream in the east of France with his amazing wife of over twenty years, Karine, and their wonderful daughter, Morgane.

Contact Patrice Maurer via https://linktr.ee/pakamosolutions

CHAPTER 19

Higher Way Of Life

By Patty Carson

As I was driving from a long, life-altering business trip, I turned into a gas station to grab a snack, only to realize I was getting ready to drive over a big curve. At that moment, I jerked the steering wheel to turn back into my lane. It was so fast; the next thing I heard was a semi-truck honking its horn at me. I have no explanation except that it was a miracle that it didn't run right over the top of me! What I know is, at that moment, I was sure I wasn't sitting there for very long, but it felt as if a lifetime of memories and thoughts went flooding through my head.

My first thought was, "Oh my gosh! Just a few hours ago, I had a young girl riding with me who was going through a troubling time. She shared that she had seriously thought of taking her life twice but decided that next time she would just pull in front of a semi. I completely empathized with her because several years of hard knocks life threw at me made her story mine as well. Twice before, I had been rock bottom, and decided that next time, I would just pull in front of a semi and be done. At that moment, I felt, she was placed in my life for a reason, and I was called to something bigger than me!"

They say your life flashes before you in your last moments. I felt that is exactly what happened at that moment in time! In my early years, my parents and I lived in Oklahoma. Life had been fairly simple until the seventh grade. That was when I really learned that life isn't always fair. Until this time, my dad had been a tile setter. That was until his knee started swelling. One day, he couldn't even hold a cigarette in his hand. You pretty much needed your knees and hands to do his job. Now, his career was over, and we were financially broke. I vividly remember Mom and Dad picking me up from grandma and grandpa's farm in Kansas on a Friday. When we got home, they were fighting over money. My dad said he was going to hustle some pool with the last remaining $75. Mom was distraught and began crying. She grabbed a bottle of pills and went into her bedroom. I went to sleep, crying and thinking that she would be dead by the morning. Instead, she woke me up in the middle of the night to have my dad talk to me. He was obviously drunk and said, 'I've been out dancing, and I spent all of our money.' That was when my parents told me they were getting divorced, and they brought me to stay on my grandparents' farm in Kansas until they settled things out. Instead of getting divorced, Mom and Dad decided to stay together, and they moved to Kansas. This was my first lesson of "Tough times don't last, but tough people do!"

My parents taught me many life lessons. I know it wasn't easy for them to stay together. They were handed many hard knocks, but they neither gave up nor quit on each other! Obviously, they weren't perfect, but they instilled me with good lessons. We went to church every Sunday. They taught me the most important book one could read was the Bible. They also taught me to pray, to believe in God and miracles.

My parents got involved in network marketing when I was nine years old, so I was raised with this attitude of "If you can believe it, with hard work, you can achieve it!" They taught me the power of our dreams! We always had personal development books, and we listened to motivational tapes, which also helped mold my mind.

Growing up, grandpa was my hero. I remember telling him, 'When you die, I am going to die because I can't ever live without you!'

I was twenty-four when I lost him, and this is where I learned a vital lesson about our thoughts and words and the power of life and death. Growing up Lutheran, we pick a Bible verse to follow us throughout our lives. Grandpa had lung cancer; he suffered in the hospital for exactly ten days, after which he died. After he died, I learned about the Bible verse he picked: "Fear none of those things which thou shalt suffer: behold, the devil shall cast *some* of you into prison, that ye may be tried; and ye shall have tribulation ten days: be thou faithful unto death, and I will give thee a crown of life" (Revelation 2:10). After learning his verse, I thought to myself, "Why would you pick a verse like that?" This was the time I reflected on my confirmation verse: "Ask and it will be given to you; seek and you will find; knock and the door will be opened to you" (Matthew 7:7). When I chose that verse, I remember thinking, 'If I have this verse, I will have everything I want in life!' Not quite true. There have been numerous trials and tribulations. But ultimately, I am blessed. After hearing grandpa's verse and how it came to fruition, I became obsessed with the power of our words.

I reflected on the time I met my husband Mark, and I told my mom when I was in the eighth grade, 'I'm going to marry him someday! He needs to grow up first, but I'm going to marry him someday!' At the age of twenty, I got married to him. While pregnant with my son, whenever anyone asked, 'Do you want a boy or a girl?' I would reply, 'I'm having a brown-eyed boy!' Guess what I got: a brown-eyed boy. I never made those proclamations with my two daughters, who have blue and hazel eyes.

What attracted me to my husband was that he was a dreamer! While dating, he built a dream that we would be retired millionaires by the time we were thirty. I believed him! However, four months after we got married, his father passed away, and I watched the light in his eye disappear, and his dreams slip away. The dream didn't stop for me. Knowing it was going to be a hard road, I was determined to make him believe again!

My first real understanding of networking was when I ran for County Treasurer. I ran a hard race; I was eight months pregnant with my oldest daughter, and I was tired. So, I decided I had done all I could the weekend before the primary. I lost by nine votes! I learned a very hard but crucial lesson. I gave up before the job was done. Had I gone all-out that weekend, I have no doubt I would have won. This was also the time that my grandpa was on his deathbed. The night before he died, he told me, "If you run a write-in campaign, you will win!" Two weeks before the election, I announced a write-in campaign. I networked with one hundred people to help me, and we won by over 200 votes. I say "we" because it was networking at its finest and teamwork made that happen!

I loved that job, but not the politics, so I started my business ventures. I was building a network marketing business with my husband. Our up-line lied to us, and my husband was done. Like most start-ups, I started a traditional business and was bankrupt within three years. After several failed attempts, I started raising dogs. I lost money there as well. I finally joined another company and made my way to the top. Finally, I felt like I had a big win, only to have the rug pulled out from under me by a new CEO who was a retired two-star general and ran the company more like a military base than a volunteer army. My business eventually crumbled. My husband was so negative by this point; he didn't believe in me or my dreams anymore. I couldn't really blame him. My kids were all grown by this point, and I believed I had shown them nothing but failure. However, deep down, I didn't believe that because I remember my son writing "I am a Winner" on the top of every paper in grade school. The teachers would often reply with a smiley face or "Yes you are" on the top of his assignment!

Still very broken and unbelieving of my dreams coming true anymore, I got a call one day from my friend Andi, who told me, 'You need to pray about it, get up, dream again, and meet the founders of the company!' I did just that, and there I went again with another business venture. Why did I do this again, possibly setting myself up for more heartbreaks? I was stubborn and wanted to prove, once again, to my family that I could win. In order to not quit, I would say a prayer each morning before getting out of bed, 'Please, God. Bring in the people I am supposed to talk to, and I will do my job!' I believe the only way you really win in life is to have a servant's heart. You don't win alone; you win by helping others win! Before getting out of bed every morning, I would say, 'I'll be here a year from today!' I have a daily positive affirmation that I say: 'I have blessings coming from every direction, I don't know from where or why, but I will accept them and thank the Lord for them!'

One of the most valuable words of advice I was ever given is: "Don't compare yourself; run your own race!" It took me six years to hit the top position of my company! After learning that a goal without a deadline is just a wish, I proclaimed: 'By June 1, 2015, I will be at the top position of our company!' I made it! Next, I heard of an incentive trip to Costa Rica. I told my husband, 'We're going to Costa Rica!' He laughed. A few months later, we were in Costa Rica! The power of our words is more than we can imagine.

The following year, I said, 'We are going to be six-figure income earners in the company!' In July of 2016, one of my biggest dreams came true! We were going to be recognized as new $100K ring earners. We invited our kids to the event. My husband said all along that he was not going to talk. As our names were announced to come up on stage, my husband said, 'I'm talking first!' He took the mic and turned to the founders of the company, thanked them, and said he was glad I listened to them because we would have probably been one of those couples who wouldn't have made it. Then he looked at me and said, in front of 3,000 people, and most importantly, our three kids, 'I'm going to let the one who built this talk now: MY HERO!' These were the moments that flashed through my mind in those few seconds sitting in front of the semi. I had found my happy place and no longer had those thoughts. However, as I drove on, I thought, 'Man, Mark calling me his hero wasn't the end of my story!'

Since that time, I have had more hard balls thrown at me with my parents, a sudden tragic loss of my son-in-law leaving my youngest daughter widowed with two young children, and my 105-year-old grandma coming to live with me for nine months during her final journey in life. Life isn't always easy, but the lessons I learned from my 105-year-old grandma gave me the courage and confidence to become vulnerable, to share my story and her story, and to give hope. Stay tuned for the full book and, as Paul Harvey would say, 'The rest of the story!'

BIOGRAPHY

Patty Carson is a professional business builder and network marketer with thirty-five years of experience. She won a write-in election when she was just twenty-four years old. She is a Nutritious Life Master Certified Coach. Patty has been featured in *Success From Home* magazine. She takes her experiences in life and business seriously and uses them to help people. Patty's passion is to inspire individuals to overcome the obstacles that hold them back and she teaches them to create a blueprint of their dreamlife. Patty has been a student of the hard-knocks university and has overcome problems using personal and leadership development for over forty years. Patty has professionally built herself to top leadership positions with two companies bringing millions in revenue to those companies and touching thousands of lives. Patty married her high school sweetheart Mark in 1984, and they share a son, two daughters, and four grandchildren.

Contact Patty Carson via https://linktr.ee/patty_carson

CHAPTER 20

From Fear To Faithfulness

By Philip Booth

Rewinding back to the mid-1980s, I found myself standing on the main street of my hometown Te Puke in New Zealand. Although having only one main street, Te Puke has now become host to the main production of Kiwifruit in New Zealand and is exported worldwide. In 1933, Jim McLoughlin began to grow 'Chinese Gooseberries' and saw its potential as a marketable fruit by renaming it Kiwifruit. In that main street, as I stood outside a small home appliance store, which had been there since I completed my apprenticeship as a radio and TV serviceman in the mid-sixties in an adjacent store across the road, I said to myself, "I'd love to own this shop," little did I know what was in store for me. At that point, I was unaware that the voice inside me came from my own spirit as I didn't feature God in my life that much, let alone know we are spirit, soul, and body. I'd sometimes attend church during Easter and other occasions; however, God was not an important part of my life at that time. In retrospect, however, God was "on my case," and I unknowingly needed Him well before I acknowledged Him and his presence and had invited Him into my life.

Since I was about twenty-two, I had a desire to own a business. I desired to make a lot of money, even to become a millionaire. However, fear, a bad self-image, lack of self-worth and confidence, plus a low sense of achievement barred me from doing so. I even lacked the courage to do things my friends did, like surfing, as I was a poor swimmer.

Life was miserable right from when I started school. I recall one nasty teacher scolding me, striking me with her bony hands, saying she wasn't happy with my effort. I found learning difficult and considered myself a "dumb" boy. I did have some musical ability and learned to play the guitar. But I found it hard to practice as I had little real application and a desire to practice and relied on the fact that I had a natural gift in music to get by. When I was around ten years old, one of my teachers, who was a classical guitarist, noticed my natural ability and started giving me lessons along with another pupil. The boy's lack of talent amused me, and I'd think he'd never make it. While I went lax, the boy practiced even harder. Eventually, he became one of New Zealand's best guitarists. I made very little progress compared to him. Later in life, I reflected that one needs to hone their God-given talents and gifts with long hours of consistent practice. Even so, I did learn enough to join several bands in my youth as a rhythm guitarist, one of the bands was called "The Arms & Legs."

After I left high school in the sixties, I did an apprenticeship as a radio serviceman and progressed to television servicing, where my love for home appliances began to develop. I worked in the service division of a company that sold home appliances. In 1972, after completing my apprenticeship, I married my sweetheart of five years and worked in that same company for some years. However, I still desired to own my own business.

One day, I saw an advertisement for a television serviceman and an offer to buy into the business by a company located in a pulp and paper town near my hometown. The fact that I could buy into the business sparked my interest. I successfully interviewed for the job and shifted to the nearby town called Kawerau. I took my Mark 1 Ford Zephyr, my Triumph Saint motorbike, my Volkswagen car, and a piano with me. I joined the service company and began servicing the TV's around the area while my business partner serviced the refrigeration appliances. I was really attracted to the possibility of buying into the business. So that's what I did and then began working hard. Some years later, I talked my business partner into opening a retail home appliance store; I ran the retail department while he ran the service division. Despite my lack of retail experience, we did well but often had cash-flow problems and sometimes had to hold cheques back for payment, sometimes up to three months.

Being married, the babies started to arrive. Having three boys made my "hell-fear" even worse as I grappled with a father's responsibilities alongside my work. Then I failed, I did something very unwise, which troubled me greatly, and I fell into depression.

Life became even more hellish, and I felt my whole character was being challenged. I slept poorly as I had a hard time coming to terms with how I had failed. I was not handling things well and relied on tranquilizers every day. I joined a service club that did good work around town, trying to be someone. Personally, this didn't help my character much, but I made many friends.

Meanwhile, the Baptist church in town began to pray for the town's businesspeople, and the Pastor often purchased electronic bits and pieces from me. The Pastor and his congregation began praying for me. As they did, God began to draw me to him. For the first time, I began thinking of questions such as:

What is reality?

What is the meaning of life?

What is the purpose of my life?

Why am I here?

When I walked around the CDB in Kawerau, at times, I would come across Christian tracts lying on the ground. Reading them showed me how I could get in touch with God through his son Jesus Christ. I came across a Christian woman who had quite a testimony of her personal salvation. She shared scriptures with me. So, besides my bed one night, I prayed along the lines suggested in the tract and asked Jesus to come into my life and forgive all my sins. A weight fell off my shoulders, and the light seemed to increase in the room. I stepped out into the night, looked up into the sky, and it was as if the heavens were revealing the presence of God. What an experience!

God's love flooded my soul.

I realized my purpose, my calling, and my self-worth.

A new chapter had begun in my life, and I felt like I wanted to return to my hometown. My business partner at the time accepted that I wanted to leave the business and bought out my shares in the company that we had started together.

I returned to Te Puke in 1983 and joined a church, being highly active in the music department and preaching also and where I remain to this day. The original Pastors, now deceased, were responsible for much of my training as a Christian.

Once back in Te Puke, I reached out to God, asking if it was His will that I go back into business again. As I prayed, I realized I was trying to make a deal with Him. So, I left the decision in His hands and hoped that He'd give me a sign. The next day, I went to a store downtown, where I found a Christian book stand. My eyes caught a book (whose name I forget) written by Televangelist Dr. Robert Schuller, the creator of Hour of Power. As I began to read the phrases of positivity, I felt God's affirmation.

Then, I headed to the company where I had done my apprenticeship for a scheduled interview as I had been offered a job there earlier that week. I took the owner's absence as God's will and left, thinking that the job was not for me. So, I headed to the shop whose owner wanted to sell out. This was the same shop I had stood in front of and had felt a tug in my heart to own, and right now, I felt the current owner's willingness to do so was God's will for me to buy the business. So, I decided on it, but not without some fear. It was as though I became double-minded for a while a few days later. I discussed it with my brother, and he commented about my "getting cold feet." I recognized it for what it was and went on to complete the purchase. Buying the business cost $18,000, as it had been run down by the previous owner who had problems with it. I prayed that I'd be able to pay the bills on the 20th of every month. I'm now happy to say that was never an issue.

I was quite apprehensive on my first day, but I got through, thanking God quietly in my office at the end of the day. The peace from this assured me that owning this business was God's approval to go back into business.

During this time, I was still with my first wife, with whom I had three children. Eventually, because of the damage I had caused to our relationship, she left me, leaving me with our sons for a time; however, being a good mother, she would spend time with them on the weekends. This was in early 1984, and by 1986, despite asking God to reunite us, I was divorced. God never goes against the will of anyone, and so my marriage was not restored. Committed to Jesus, I then focused on letting him speak through the Bible to me. Over the next ten years, God allowed me to dig out many negative aspects of my life. I'm happy to report I'm not anything like my old negative self. Thank God for that!

Over time, my shop became way too small due to God's blessings, as I had learned the scriptural principles of giving. I found a bigger building three shops away. It housed a much bigger shop area, two other smaller shops on the bottom floor, and three shops upstairs. This was a huge opportunity for me, with real potential to grow. Under God's direction and via some help from a financier, I made an offer for the building. It was accepted. However, the seller wanted me to add the

GST (10% of the price negotiated at the time). My financier agreed on the exceptional deal, and I got the bigger building complete with existing tenants. The GST content came back to me, which I spent on refurbishing the area. People were amazed at our opening. They sent flowers and letters, and some appreciated that I restored a rundown building, today worth over one million dollars. My original loan is long paid-off. I have a mortgage-free home and a rental property short of a few payments before it's mine.

My business experienced growth, along with some trials, especially during the financial crash of 2008. Despite a devalued bottom line, I did not lay anyone off. God remained faithful and heard my prayers. At times where I'd be short ($30,000) on the month's bills, my good friend and employee Tom and I prayed together; and the money was always there. Tom and I enjoyed many years together (1984-2015), praying at the start of the business day and thanking God at the end of the day for prosperity in our business, region, our families, and the families of all those who worked there. In November of 2010, the news that Kiwifruit canker (Psa) had been found in an orchard in Te Puke went viral as it threatened the viability of Kiwifruit in New Zealand as it could have completely wiped out every existing vine and destroyed the multimillion-dollar industry as it had already done in other nations. Being a severe threat to our area and retail sector and, of course, my own business, I inquired of the Lord. His reply was to say, "I am going to bless the Kiwifruit Industry." To make a long story short, he did, and the Kiwifruit Industry continues to thrive, which is another proof of God's love and faithfulness for people.

In 2013, my desire for marriage was stronger than ever, so I went to Nanning, China, to meet a Chinese lady. I stayed there for a couple of weeks, getting to know her, which was difficult as she knew very little English, and I, very little Mandarin. Nevertheless, we still liked each other. I returned to New Zealand to get her into the country. But it never worked out. I read this as an indication from God that He had other plans for me.

In 2014, I fell into depression after having surgery done on my prostate for cancer. This bout of depression taught me why people are driven to suicide. For myself, I couldn't understand why, even as a Christian and God in my life, I was so depressed. I thought it would never pass as everything seemed dark, but I didn't come close to suicide. To make things worse, I had an employee who tried to take me over, telling me he prayed to God for this to happen. His manipulative attitude made my life difficult. I'm happy to say nothing transpired. However, over the years, I've had many awesome people work for me, and we've all had great relationships that exist to this day.

Returning to my birthplace made me realize that God has a plan for our lives and even a geographical place in mind. Relationships with the right people are crucial to that plan's working. With God's help, I've been able to serve my community through my work. Even before the COVID-19 pandemic, more so during and after, people wanted to "shop local" and were eager to see that I did not shut down. I remember reading years ago that the benchmark for greatness in business is gauged in the level of service given to their customers.

I've been in business since 1983 when it went through various names: Phil Booth TV & Audio; Phil Booth Appliance Court; Phil Booth Retravision; and Phil Booth Appliance Spot. My current retail business is called "100% Phil Booth." Being seventy now, I feel like I'm only getting started and have no intention of retiring. I still enjoy my business immensely.

After waiting on God from 1986, after my divorce, to 2018 for a wife of His choosing, He brought along a beautiful Vietnamese woman with two children aged thirteen and ten. We are so happy and compatible that my heart swells with joy. She was well worth waiting for. My parents have passed away, but hers are still alive and only a few years younger than me. I have gained two stepsons, some parents-in-law, two more brothers-in-law, and their families, all based in Hanoi.

Additionally, I have eight grandchildren from my own family. My new wife and I were married on 6 October 2018, and a year later, she found she had nasopharyngeal cancer. But that's another story!

From fear to faithfulness: the faithfulness I refer to is God's faithfulness to those who have committed their lives to Him despite feelings of helplessness and failure. God vivifies that which otherwise might have been destroyed, and He delights being part of people's lives—His creation. He says, "Delight yourself in the Lord . . . and He will give the desires of your heart."

The Bible says, "A faithful man who can find?" Yet, in God, faithfulness is possible. All is accomplished by faith. Fear is the total absence of faith. Every day in God is a fresh start.

"Commit your way to the Lord, and He will cause your thoughts to come in line with His will, and so shall your plans be established and succeed." God always leads us to victory. Because of this fact, 1983 was indeed a brand new start in life for me, and the fears that dogged me in my early life have left for good, all due to God's faithfulness. Even the fear of lack has left me as God proved his faithfulness in that area by ensuring that I always had sufficient to pay my bills, and that was an answer to prayer. My DREAM to own my own business came into reality by daring to believe God and trusting in his faithfulness.

BIOGRAPHY

Philip Booth is the proprietor and CEO of 100% Phil Booth. He has been a retailer of home appliances for forty years. His career began after completing his Trade Certificate as a radio and television serviceperson, after which he launched a career in retailing. He has owned and managed two businesses, and his longevity has resulted from leveraging the two top appliance co-operating companies in New Zealand and a strong faith in the goodness of God. He currently belongs to the Appliance Connexion Group Services Ltd, which is associated with the NARTA Group of Australasia. Phil has kept up with current appliance retailing trends by traveling extensively to conferences hosted by various groups and suppliers of appliance brands, CEOs, visits to appliance factories, and listening to motivational guest speakers.

Contact Philip Booth via https://linktr.ee/philbooth

CHAPTER 21

Growing A Side Business Into A Full-Time Income

By Phillipa Nanyondo Byamah

I stood behind the stage as the MC bellowed out my short bio over the microphone while the crowd of thousands eagerly awaited what I had to say. At that moment, I wondered if it really could be me they were waiting for. If it *was* me in the wings, waiting to step onto this big international stage with members from different countries, how on earth had I arrived at that point? Was it really me, ready to teach, inspire, and share my story? You see, no one would have believed a few years ago that I would have gotten so far, as my journey had always seemed to be one of going against the odds. It started with faith as small as a mustard seed—and a little determination.

As a child, I always wanted to do something with my life and feared not having the choices I needed to succeed. I had seen both worlds of having and not having a lot. And I trusted the God I serve who says we are made to thrive, not to survive.

Growing up in a family of eight children, four boys and four girls, my father taught us that working hard for what we wanted to achieve was the key to success. He endeavored to educate us at the best schools in the country and sacrificed everything in his power to ensure we had the best in life. During my secondary and high school education, it soon became apparent I possessed a natural gift for scientific subjects and had a keen liking for and ability to solve mathematical problems. Later on, taking on a BSc in Quantitative Economics on a government sponsorship also proved easy for me. Indeed, that young girl slowly grew out of her playfulness and began taking her academic performance very seriously. It surprised my parents that I was regularly at the top of my class, especially in math exams.

I started my first job in the banking industry, even before fully graduating. My keen eye for detail and enthusiasm for learning about what went on in the different departments saw me being regularly promoted, ending up in the credit department. I also moved banks in pursuit of a more satisfying professional career. As I pursued more goals in life, I started to tell myself that doing even more was possible. As a wise person said, "The first step towards getting somewhere is to decide that you are not going to stay where you are."

I started my first 'side hustle' shortly after I joined the corporate world. I had quickly embarked on saving a good percentage of my small salary, and I pondered where to invest it most profitably. After accumulating some funds, I launched a special car hire business: I bought a second-hand vehicle that wasn't in good mechanical condition.

My first lesson: If you think of an idea, don't wait for a 'perfect time' to put it into action. Just take the first step and get started. There's never a perfect time or perfect conditions. Just start with whatever you have and take a leap of faith. Also, learn to start small, as from small and humble beginnings come greater things. In my case, by starting early in coming up with different ideas for creating avenues of earning an additional income, I used the vital lesson of taking the first step of faith and starting anyway. I didn't wait for perfect conditions, and neither did I wait to have a lot of money; I just got started with what I had. And that started my journey of learning from my business mistakes.

"Courage isn't about knowing the path,
it's about taking the first step."[21]

—Katie Davis

I hired out the vehicle I'd bought for someone to drive it as a taxi, and they were supposed to pay me a certain amount of money weekly, although I would cover the mechanical and servicing costs. This worked well for the first few weeks until the 'stories' from the driver as to why he couldn't pay me started and seemed endless. From one mechanical failure to another, I soon found that I was shelling out more in repair and servicing costs than I had revenue coming in. Reluctantly, I decided I had to give up that particular dream and let the car go.

Next, I started a motorbike business, where I bought a new bike and hired it out in almost the same arrangement as with the previous car business. In my country, Uganda, motorcycle transport can be lucrative, as bikes ease transportation in congested city centers. But I soon began to get the same 'stories' from the motorcycle driver as I had from the taxi driver, and the epitome was when police confiscated the motorbike over some breach of traffic rules. The procedure to resolve the issue was not only lengthy but also costly and, once again, I soon had to give it up.

My lesson number two: Before embarking on any business, consult experts in that area. I ventured into the transport business, which I knew for sure could be lucrative, without first getting any advice from a successful special hire (taxi) operator. Neither did I consult anyone who was successful in the motorcycle business. I relied on hearsay, and soon I was learning on the job—the hard way. The people I picked to partner with me took advantage of my partial ignorance, which meant my initial,

---

21 "'Courage Isn't about Knowing the Path, It's about Taking the First Step.'" Katie Davis Quote. Accessed September 15, 2021. https://quotefancy.com/quote/1723942/Katie-Davis-Courage-isn-t-about-knowing-the-path-it-s-about-taking-the-first-step.

unsuccessful forays into business became the first lessons learned on my side business journey.

Identifying my next business venture was not difficult: I have always been a busy person who won't settle for less than I think is right. I always endeavored to complete my daily workload, tasks, and even projects before their deadlines, and I would soon be asking, 'What's next?'

The habit of keeping aside part of my salary as savings for future investments enabled this journey of growing my part-time businesses into full-time income sources. **And this makes my lesson number three:** *there are many times when we have big ideas and want to jump in to realize them (without experience) in a similarly big way. Lack of starting capital should never be an excuse not to start a business; if you believe in what you're doing, then make it happen by putting aside some savings to enable your dream to come true.*

We need to realize that whereas it's good to save, you have to learn to let your money grow and, in turn, allow it to work for you. Before you identify and embark on a business that you will invest in for a better return, it is advisable not to have your savings sited long on a savings accounts but rather invest it in other avenues that will give you a better return like fixed deposits, government instruments like Treasury bills and bonds, umbrella trust funds and other Insurance packages among others. That way, your money earns more for you, interest is compounded, and you start earning more in interest on your original deposit. Never underestimate the value of money and time, taking on Life Assurance plans or education plans (if you have children) will save you so much in the future. This is a hustle-free way of getting your net worth to increase, one shilling after another. Recognize the compounding power of money— **that was my lesson number four.**

I have an eye for <u>turning passions, talent, pain, and gaps in the market into opportunities</u>. My next business venture was one I started because of my husband's love for popcorn. He loved fresh popcorn so much that I wanted to ensure he could always enjoy this treat whenever he wanted to. But our nearest supermarket didn't have a fresh popcorn machine, and I saw an opportunity to regularly supply my husband with fresh popcorn and make some extra income from the business idea of having a fresh popcorn machine at our local supermarket. I learned two lessons from this venture:

Lesson five: *Opportunities to make money are around you. You just have to look with 'smart eyes,' and you will see them.*

Lesson six: *Never undermine a job that will earn you an extra income. Often, we suffer from the 'I am too cool' syndrome—wrongly thinking that some jobs are not meant for a certain class of people.*

Although I was already working in the banking sector and climbing the corporate ladder, I had no shame about taking on a fresh popcorn business. After a short time of supplying fresh popcorn to this one supermarket, doors soon opened to all its other outlets, and I found myself supplying other items to their outlets all across the country and in their Kenyan outlets as well. So, I approached two other supermarkets and expanded my supply chain. The money I earned through this venture meant we could easily pay our monthly expenses without touching our regular salaries.

In 2016, after a long December break spent in the traditional activities of visiting grannies and family, which we loved doing, we set out to do something different by deciding to have a family vacation. I had always loved travel, and I felt we needed to start living life with our kids and creating some different kinds of memories. After doing lots of research, this dream landed me in my next adventure, which would allow me to travel the world and gain an extra-income stream derived from multi-level marketing techniques. Of course, I didn't hesitate, given that working on any project I was passionate about was bound to be enjoyable. I learned that business models were changing, and companies were using MLM or word of mouth to get the word out about their products and services.

I decided to embark on this business and learn everything I needed by finding appropriate coaches and mentors to follow. It's important to follow people who have what you want and then do exactly what they do to become like them. I decided to get into student mode and learn as much as I could from my virtual mentors. I was coachable and trainable and applied everything I learned. I also found an accountability partner, with whom I shared my goals and visions, and I was held accountable for the daily activities and tasks I was supposed to fulfill.

Have you ever wondered how some people have this ability to handle many tasks at the same time and do all of them quite well?

Well, I tried to master the art and science of personal effectiveness. With the determination I had to succeed, I knew I first had to understand how to segment daily tasks and activities and prioritize important things directly related to achieving my visions and goals. I started slowly cutting back on certain activities that I realized had been taking up a lot of my time but were not actively contributing to my bigger goals. I became more intentional with life, as I tried to squeeze as much out of each day as possible to be more productive and effective. By doing a lot in the short time allotted to me for the day, I also learned how to delegate and empower people. I began to utilize the strong support system surrounding me. From home to my formal workplace and my side businesses, what became evident to me was that working alone, I could travel fast, but by standing on the shoulders of giants, I could go much further and also see farther. Based on this, I started to help people in my organization, and the more I helped others, the more I became better and saw better results for myself.

So, that day as I stood behind the stage as the host and Master of Ceremonies for the day bellowed my name, inviting me to come up on the stage and share my life experiences about how I got to the top of my organization and succeeded in turning my side business into a full-time income that helped me build my retirement portfolio, I pondered once more the past years of struggle and hard work, the sleepless nights of planning, the long meetings, the endless phone calls, meeting clients, attending training sessions, then driving through traffic jams to get home late, often way past the bedtimes of my beautiful children. I knew for sure I had sacrificed a lot to get to where I was. And I knew that there is always a trade-off in life and that, for me to break through and succeed in ensuring my family's future security and comfort, nothing was more important than making those positive life changes.

BIOGRAPHY

Phillipa Nanyondo Wavamunno Byamah is an economist, banker, public speaker, performance specialist, entrepreneur, and business coach. She is an independent-minded, self-motivated, and versatile professional who seeks and achieves purpose-filled results in sometimes uncertain circumstances. Phillipa's enormous potential to thrive, to lead others, and her willingness to help others achieve their highest potential has been her calling in life. While rising in both her banking and business careers, she has traveled extensively to speak and motivate others, always striving to give of her best in their service, and has been rewarded with numerous related accolades, including achieving the top rank of her network marketing company. Her visionary leadership has mentored many around her, allowing them to experience great business and life success. She endeavors to leave a little piece of herself everywhere she goes. She lives in Uganda with her husband, Raymond Karuhanga Byamah, and her two adorable children, Nahereza (God gives) and Kansiimeruhanga (I give thanks to God).

Connect with Phillipa Nanyondo Wavamunno Byamah
via https://linktr.ee/phillipawavah

CHAPTER 22

Finish What You Start

By Regina Nunnally

In 1987, I was in Tae Kwon Do for quite a while, about four years or so. I wanted to quit, but I was genuinely scared to tell my father. I dreaded the tongue-lashing I would receive. But I didn't care; my heart wasn't in it. I was simply going through the motions. This situation went on for a few weeks, before I finally mustered enough courage to tell my daddy the truth. All that day at school, it was on my mind; my heartbeat speeded up, and my head started hurting when I thought about it. This was the day I was going to tell my father I wanted to quit going to Little Dragons Tae Kwon Do Center. What explanation would I give? How could I make things sound so bad that he would go along with it?

I got home, and he came out to take me to class. I told him flat out, "Daddy, I want to quit." There it was; I'd said it. The sky didn't come crashing down and, to my surprise, my daddy didn't say a word. It was opposite to what I'd expected. He wasn't all hail, fire, and brimstone. He simply said, "Okay." What? My daddy was not tripping over me for quitting?

I felt relieved, but then he said, "But you have to give back all the trophies, certificates, belts, and medals you've earned." Huh? Did he just say give back the trophies I'd won in tournaments, the Certificates of Achievement I'd received for training with some of the best martial arts teachers around, the belts I'd earned sparring with my instructor, who was a professional kick-boxer? I immediately recalled all the black eyes, chipped teeth, sprained fingers and toes, the jammed jawbone, and the shin knots I'd received in training. It was as though I again felt all those painful moments and emotions attached to these precious memorials.

I asked him why. He answered, "Because you won't want anything to remind you of the fact that you quit." Boom! There it was. I heard the disappointment in his voice, but I also heard regret. You see, my father dropped out of school when he was in the tenth grade. Over the years, he attempted to launch numerous businesses, all of which failed. There were probably more things he wished he'd done but hadn't—because when it got hard, he quit. So, in a way, he was living through me. He saw potential in me that I didn't see. Then he said, "You're too close to black belt. Get your black belt and then do what you want. Do it for me." So, in December 1988, I received my black belt. It was a big deal—I did it for my daddy. Then, in May 1989, the day after Mother's Day, my daddy died.

Challenge #1

I was sixteen and a junior at Mainland Senior High School when my dad left my mama and me behind. We had his homegoing service the following Saturday morning. I went to my junior prom that same evening. I didn't feel like going but was encouraged to go by my peers. Plus, I could hear my daddy saying, "One monkey doesn't stop the show." He never got to see me dressed up, looking pretty. That was one of the hardest days of my life. I buried my father that morning and attended the junior prom that same evening.

Challenge #2

During my senior year, I accepted some terrible advice from my school counselor. I was on track to graduate Cum Laude. My grades during the first semester of my senior year would be the determining factor in maintaining that track. I was eligible to apply for a scholarship, but I needed classes to be competitive. So, I rearranged my schedule. I took physics, honors chemistry, and trigonometry to qualify. I totally bombed it. I was so close and had worked so hard for almost four years, and then one semester took me out of the game. My grade point average dropped. When my friends got their caps and gowns and honor cords, I did not get mine. One of them even asked me where mine were. "Denied," I said; I'd missed the mark. But my father's words still rang in my ears—"Finish what you start!" The second semester was better, but it was too late. I graduated with honors, but I had missed the mark for graduating Cum Laude. That experience left a bitter aftertaste in my mouth. I felt robbed and cheated. I felt defeated, but I decided in my heart to finish what I started as best as I could.

Challenge #3

I decided to go to law school. To apply, you must take the law school admissions test or LSAT. However, out of ignorance, I didn't take it seriously enough. I underestimated the difficulty entirely. My 'friend' was pursuing the same course as me, but we never really shared much. So, I guess it was all on me. I studied the day before, walked in, took the test, and did miserably—ending up with a low score. However, I thought I still had a shot at getting into my alma mater, the University of Florida, so I applied. My friend applied and was accepted. I was denied admission. I applied to four other schools, who also rejected my applications.

I took the LSAT twice after that. In the middle of the second test, my brain started to freeze up. I'd read a paragraph, then start losing my concentration. The words on the paper wouldn't make sense to me, which had never happened before. In the end, I'd walked out of the test early, lying to the proctor by telling her I was sick. I cried on the way home.

Then, one day, a revelation came to me: I figured that I would stay motivated by surrounding myself with reminders of what I wanted to achieve. So, I contacted several law offices and volunteered my services. The local legal aid office accepted my invitation, and I volunteered to interview potential clients. Then, the director suggested I talk to a local judge. I arranged that, and the judge became my mentor. Being around the very thing I was pursuing, studying law, kept me focused. During the third testing, I met a guy who gave me an application form for a new law school opening in Orlando. I applied and, in May 1997, I received my admissions letter to attend The University of Orlando School of Law.

Challenge #4

Studying for the bar meant working anywhere between six to eight hours a day, although the rules have changed significantly now. Back then, there were eight subjects to review. The test was in two parts of six hours each. That meant twelve hours in total, with two days reading and answering two-hundred questions and writing essays. The bar test is so extreme that they even have EMS standing by on the scene. I became a bar rep, running study sessions, so I could afford to take the exam. I watched the training videos during the day, then my roommate and I would watch them again at night. Before taking the real bar exam, I took two practice exams. I needed a 131 to pass; I made a 128 on the real exam. I failed! Couldn't they have found three more points? It was so frustrating.

So, I asked God for a plan to succeed, and this is what He showed me: I should start with my weakest subject first, which was Evidence. I read the section and did all the practice questions. Then, I went on to my next weakest subject, property, reading the material, and adding more practice questions. I was soon walking around with a stack of index cards filled with questions and answers that I took everywhere I went. I even studied them in church, in the choir, during a sermon.

Before I studied, I prayed Joshua 1:9, which says, "Be strong, be of good courage . . . the Lord God is with you wherever you go."

On the day of the exam, which lasted three hours, I flew through the first part comprising one-hundred questions. My studying meant I could see patterns in the questions that made the answers flow like a stream. I finished early and walked out jubilant. I was blown away.

After lunch, I sat down, ready to knock out the second half of the exam. I prayed my scripture, got working, but then hit a brick wall. About every third or fourth question, I got stuck. I started to feel a little anxious. I struggled through the second half and didn't finish early that time. For two long months, I waited on the results. When the day finally came, my heart was pounding because it was do or die for me. The results were being posted on the bar website, so I signed in. And there it was—I'd passed. When I received my letter in the mail, my score was 147, more than enough to pass the exam.

Life Lessons

First, never underestimate your plans to meet your goals. You need to take it seriously. I realized in my early years that I was not preparing myself properly to meet my goals. Partly due to ignorance and arrogance. I heard someone say that blame is a way to discharge pain and discomfort. I can't blame anyone else for my shortcomings and take ownership of them. If you enjoy eating humble pie, I strongly recommend sticking to the plan. Success is in your hands!

Second, learn how to encourage yourself. No matter how hard, no matter how ugly it seems, remember the words of those who have your best interests at heart. I challenge you to speak the words over your life—you must allow the inspiration of others to penetrate your heart. But be careful not to take pain as your guide; if you do, the antidote to your situation won't work. Your heart will become hard and nothing good will be able to take root there. Remember, a closed mind does not get fed.

Third, take action. People spoke into my life. I took action. I received revelations from God in the middle of my dry moments. I took action. The word of encouragement came; I took action. I got advice and direction; I took action. All those years ago, when my father advised me not to quit practicing Tae Kwon Do, I took action. Remember, A-C-T-I-O-N stands for A Challenge That Includes Opportunities Now!

Fourth, learn to thrive where you're planted. Studying for the bar was tough enough, but I determined in my heart not to let it devour my soul. Failing the bar was embarrassing; however, I kept my head high and pressed on. Every time you face a challenge, don't forget to live.

Embrace the moment until your change comes. Remember, it's only a temporary setback setting you up for a permanent comeback.

In conclusion, as a lawyer for over seventeen years now, I take action for my clients with a passion that gives them confidence. I wanted the pain and disappointment to stop. Those torment times directed me to meet great people who continue to mentor me in business and encourage me to cultivate myself to become a judge. You have to keep moving, my friend. You've come too far to turn around, and you're too close to your goal to quit now.

Keep the faith and stay the course. I am rooting for you. Purpose in your heart to finish what you start!

BIOGRAPHY

Regina Nunnally is an author, criminal defense attorney, pastor, community leader, character actress, motivational speaker, and travelista entrepreneur. Born and raised in the Funshine State, Daytona Beach, Florida, Regina is a contributing author to the Amazon publishing bestseller *Daily Dose of Direction for Women in Business*. She has contributed articles to *Program Success* magazine and *Nia* magazine and collaborated on a story for an audio series called Confinement

Chronicles Volume III, presented by Angie BEE Productions. Regina has been a featured speaker at the Healing the Whole Woman Conference and is scheduled to be a featured speaker/travel expert at an upcoming engagement called Map Out Your Life 2.0 in October 2020.

Connect with Regina Nunnally via https://linktr.ee/seetheworldthrumyeyes

CHAPTER 23

Help Wanted: Hire Yourself

By Reginald Dockery

Many people dream of freedom, financial freedom, job freedom, and even time freedom. Before you dream it, I want you to contemplate the question: What is freedom? With most jobs, you're told what time to come in, what time to leave, what time to take a break, and what time to take lunch. Your employer also approves, or not, the time you can go on vacation or take personal days. Does that sound like freedom to you? There are several ways to be free, both financially and in your career path. These days, to have financial and time freedom, you will need multiple streams of income. The average millionaire has a minimum of seven streams or avenues of income.

In this chapter, I will examine many of those avenues: You can hire yourself as an employee, which is being self-employed. Then there's hiring yourself as a CEO or president, in which case, you are an owner and overseer. I'll show you how to answer the "Help Wanted" sign within you. I've heard several multimillionaires say, "You can never become wealthy or financially independent working a regular 9 to 5 job for someone else." So, I tell you to search within yourself today and answer your own "Help Wanted" sign.

We all have things we love to do. Maybe you love to write? Maybe taking photos makes you feel like a million dollars? Or perhaps you love crafting hand-made signs? I'm talking about the thing that makes you feel alive, your passion, what creates a fire in your bones.

But it's hard to believe you can ever make money from your passion. Surely, you think, I can't make money doing [insert your passion]. Nobody would pay me to do that. It's too much fun, and I love it too much. No way could I make money doing that.

That's where you're wrong. Today, thanks to the internet, almost any passion can be turned into a profitable side hustle.

Did you catch that?

You can make money doing the things you love most. Yep, you can turn your passion project into a profitable project. We all could use some extra cash in our lives. We've got bills to pay, kids to send to school, car repairs to make, and a dozen other expenses. Some extra cash could be useful and go a long way toward making our lives easier. This is where hiring yourself is crucial.

If you're interested in 'get rich quick' schemes, then this book is not for you. Because here's the reality: Creating a profitable business takes time, diligence, hard work, blood, sweat, and tears (well, hopefully, not too many tears!)

If you want to succeed with your life as a CEO, prepare to put in some work. You shouldn't expect to start operating and immediately have boatloads of cash pouring in. You need to be ready to put in many hours of work over the long-haul.

How do you generate the motivation needed to put in all that hard work? Look at your life as it currently is. Are you living your best life now? Are you completely fulfilled with your day job? Are there other things you would love to do to make money? Do you see others doing what you want to do?

If you're not living your best life now, let that serve as a motivator for your own business. You really can make money doing what you LOVE. You can generate significant income doing something that brings great satisfaction into your life.

How would it change your life if you were doing work that made you happy? How would it revolutionize things for you if you enjoyed the work you do every day?

To increase motivation for your business, envision what a successful outcome would look like for your side hustle. Paint a picture in your mind of what your best life will look like.

First, you need to get very clear on the answers to these questions:

- How badly do you want to succeed in your own company?
- What benefits do you want to experience?
- How will the extra cash you earn help you?
- What joy will you experience from doing what you love?

If you're not highly motivated to make your business a reality, it won't happen. Because here's the truth: Your Business will take you away from other good things that you could be doing.

You may need to give up some of the following:

- Watching television
- Your favorite reality shows
- Hobbies
- Spending too much time on the internet
- Time spent with friends

You may even need to sacrifice time usually spent with your family, although I don't recommend doing that over the long haul.

The point is simply that you will have to make sacrifices to make your business a reality. You're going to have to do the hard work necessary. You must be willing to give up some of the good things to achieve a great thing.

Most people don't realize that it usually takes a significant amount of time and work before you start making good money from your side hustle.

Success happens over the long haul, not overnight. If you want your business to be profitable, you must be willing to make sacrifices until you finally reach your objective.

World-famous soccer player Pele said: "Success is no accident. It is hard work, perseverance, learning, studying, sacrifice, and most of all, love of what you are doing, or learning to do." If you want to succeed, you must be willing to work hard and persevere. The good news is that if you persevere, you will almost certainly succeed.

All that being said, you must be confident that you can do it. If you constantly doubt yourself, you'll have a hard time getting traction. But if you have faith in yourself and believe firmly in your abilities, you truly can achieve great things.

The best time to start a business is right now. Don't wait any longer. There will never be a perfect time to get started. Start working on your project today, and adjust as time goes on. So, how do you identify what your business should be? How do you know what you should invest your time in? How can you determine the best activities to focus on? It's simple: You start by identifying the things you're most passionate about and interested in.

A business is the intersection of passion and profit. In other words, it's all about taking the things you love and are good at and turning them into a profitable gig. So, the first step is to identify what you love to do AND are good at doing. Both elements are required. If you want your business to be sustainable, you must love doing it. If you don't, you'll burn out quickly. When hard work and sacrifices are needed, you won't want to make them. A successful business involves an activity that you love doing.

You must also be good at your passion. In other words, you must have the necessary skill set to make it a reality. If you're not good at creating your product or performing your service, others simply won't want to pay you for it.

Ask yourself these questions:

- What do you love doing?
- What have people told you that you're good at?
- What do you lose track of time doing?
- What valuable skills do you have that people would pay for?
- What needs can you meet?

These questions will help you find the intersection of passion and profit. They will help you determine both your skillset and what you love. When these two things combine, you have a viable side hustle.

There is a psychological concept called "Flow." This is when you find yourself so immersed in an activity that you lose all track of time and are simply focused on what's in front of you. Your mind isn't distracted at all. Rather, you simply "flow" with your activity.

When do you find yourself in the "flow" of things? Pay attention to these moments. It's these activities that could be turned into sustainable companies.

Unless you're building something completely new and revolutionary, you're going to be competing against others. Whether you're selling a widget or offering coaching services, there will always be others against whom you're competing for business.

THE POWER OF LEADERSHIP

If you're going to succeed with your occupational passion, you must first find a way to differentiate yourself from your competitors. In other words, figure out how you're going to stand out from the crowd, how you're going to attract customers, how your offer is different and better than your competitor's.

How can you differentiate yourself from your competitors? There are numerous ways, including:

- Enhanced quality products or services
- Superior customer service
- Speedier delivery
- Less expensive products or services
- Higher or lower profit margins
- A noble cause you support with profits from your product

For example, let's say you're selling skin moisturizer online. You could create a unique skin moisturizer of better quality than most other skin moisturizers. Because your skin moisturizer is of better quality, you can sell it for a higher price and make higher profit margins.

Or you could sell your skin moisturizer at a discount and sell a higher volume. Or you could create an aggressive online marketing campaign designed to get your skin moisturizer ad seen by more people than your competitors.

If you don't find a way to differentiate yourself from your competitors, there's no reason why customers should purchase from you rather than them. You absolutely must find a way to stand out in the crowd.

All successful people are optimistic, and all optimistic people are usually, in one way or another, sooner or later, successful in accomplishing their life goals. Optimistic people tend to say "the glass is half-full," not "half-empty." They believe the whole universe is friendly towards them and is helping them in achieving their dreams. However, what many people tend to do is remain optimistic until they're just about to reach their goal. Then, they lose patience, become victims of criticism, and turn their back on the goal, resisting when it tries to pull them back in. This is why there isn't a success story for every dreamer or a rags-to-riches story for every poor person.

When Bill Gates was asked, if he found a dollar bill on the ground, would he bother picking it up? He said he would. Warren Buffett responded to the same question by saying that if Bill Gates missed picking up the dollar bill, he himself wouldn't. It's not as though they are hungry for money, but rather the optimistic mindset through which they perceive events that have led them to be among the world's wealthiest people today.

Wisdom of the early twentieth century:

The successful people of the early twentieth century had so much optimism that many of today's entrepreneurs regard them as their teachers, even if they haven't met them in person. For instance, W. Clement Stone has been described as a paranoid, not the type you find in an asylum, but what's called an inverse paranoid. While a classic paranoid believes the world is plotting to do him harm, Stone believed the world was plotting to do him good. He looked for opportunities in every challenging or difficult situation and used those opportunities to empower and enrich himself or advance his causes. In one of his famous books, Napoleon Hill mentioned these golden words: "Every adversity, every failure, and every heartache carries with it the seed of an equal or greater benefit."

Henry Ford was a highly optimistic entrepreneur, who believed if we think we can do a thing, or we think we can't do a thing, either way, we're all right. So, it's not the type of problem or obstacle in our way that matters but our attitude towards it that matters and determines whether we can proceed towards our goals.

But why are we all right either way, according to Ford?

In other words, the question is, does positive thinking work, or is it just a pseudo-scientific idea? If you think and believe you can't do something or can't accomplish a task within a particular time, you simply won't. However, if you think you can or constantly tell yourself you can and come to believe it, when your mind says, "Yes, you can!" then you're more likely to do the things necessary to make it happen. First, you must establish an objective or goal for your life. Success is purpose-driven. Hence, to be a successful person, you need to have precise intentions. Since we have different desires and passions, you need to figure out what yours is and discern what makes you happy, then use them as a source of motivation. Once you determine what this goal is, you can build your life-purpose around it. You can even try making a career out of something you genuinely love. Greater success is practically guaranteed if you're doing something you're genuinely passionate about. Additionally, your goals and objectives should be realistic and attainable.

Visualize yourself as a successful person. Imagining your success precisely can pave the way for easier and more effective implementation of the necessary steps toward reaching your goal. In the long run, you'll be convinced of your capacity to fulfill your goals, which in turn motivates you even more and helps you build self-confidence.

Recognize which abilities you need to hone and which elements of reaching your goal you can outsource. Skills can either be acquired naturally or after continuous learning and practice. Even if you believe you're capable of taking on several tasks at once, that approach is usually not practical because it's time-consuming and can cause you to burn out. If you have more than one undertaking at hand, the best solution may be outsourcing. Knowing how to outsource some essential tasks is essential because it helps you get more work done in the least amount of time.

Create a timeline for when you want to accomplish your goal/s. If you don't fix a specific deadline for attaining your objective, then you won't know whether you've succeeded or failed. When arranging a timetable, remember it should be demanding but also realistic and feasible at the same time.

BIOGRAPHY

Reginald Dockery is a remarkable professional and a tenacious entrepreneur specializing in business brand consultancy and public speaking. *Making it Happen Instead of Watching it Happen* is the theme statement for this influential speaker, author, and serial entrepreneur. A Detroit native, Reginald's journey in the corporate world started many years ago, and he has worked with renowned corporations, including the NAACP Detroit Chapter, TGI Friday, Lucky Strike Entertainment, United Way, and ASCAP, among many others. He helps create custom training and personal relationship development programs for his clients. His background includes gaining a Bachelor of Science degree from Full Sail University. Coupled with his experience in both the music and corporate sectors, this has enabled him to build a successful career. As the CEO of Lyfe Legacy Management and Dockery Enterprises Inc, Reginald leads his team in providing multiple consulting services, including business and personal branding, leadership, event management, and business development. Reginald's ability to build and maintain incredible working relationships has contributed significantly to his success. He maintains a track record for successfully completing multi-million-dollar projects, an outcome achieved by successfully coordinating and developing partnerships.

CHAPTER 24

Smile, See Whose Life You Can Touch

by Renee Robinson

There is another one walking down the street, smiling. Do you ever ponder and imagine why they are smiling? Do they have a secret? Some days, I think we all wish we were them and that our lives would be full of smiles.

Childhood memories can change the way you embark, restart and proceed through life. One of my favorite memories as a little girl was sitting on my father's knee early in the morning before the sun came up and he went to work. I always loved to talk—never a quiet moment in our home. We would have toast with peanut butter and jam, always turned upside down, so the peanut butter never stuck to the roof of my mouth. Dad would call me Renee Tin Tin and tell me it was okay to do things differently and be different from everyone else. "Don't be a sheep," as he put it.

Growing up in a financially underprivileged family—and as a red-headed girl—came with difficult times because of all the teasing and the rudeness from others. It didn't take long to know I was different.

My biggest downfall was learning to be strong on the inside. I had never learned about boundaries regarding how I was to be treated by others throughout my life. From a very young age, I would push any and all negative interactions away by sharing the biggest, most passionate smile with others. But I would hurt on the inside.

My dad gave me the following wisdom throughout my life: You can be and do whatever you want in life—a doctor, a teacher, or a machine operator. It does not matter if you are a man or a woman, but what does matter is you. You can't keep looking backward and waiting for others to approve. You need to give yourself the approval to be the best at whatever you want to be and move forward to the next chapter of your life.

It is you who chooses. You have the right to go after anything you want in life, but you do not have the right to expect others to help you or do it for you. That is only a bonus.

Even as a very young child, I would be a social butterfly. I would wander around and visit other farms to help people with their gardens or just say hello. I would always hear comments saying, "You are always so happy," or "You must be an old soul."

As a young woman at the age of twelve, I would skip school to go visit and help people at a local nursing home. When I returned home, I would be punished for missing school, but my father understood I had a calling to help people. My argument was that those people needed me and my smile (and I needed theirs).

When I finished school, I went to college and became a nurse working in a psychiatric unit. I loved where my life had taken me. I was energetic and passionate about helping others. Then, within moments, only eight years into my career, everything in my life changed.

On this particular morning, I had walked into a patient's room, and that's all I remember. I woke up later that day in the hospital. Confused about what had happened, someone explained to me that I had been attacked and needed surgery on my right shoulder. My arm was secured across my chest. The doctors explained that I would have a brace built for me around my torso and a sleeve brace straight out the front of me in which I'd place my arm so my shoulder would be in a neutral position to heal. When I asked how long this would be, I was told they didn't know because my shoulder and nerve damage injury was quite unique.

I remember sitting on the bedroom floor, on a long-distance call: "Dad, I can't do this anymore. I'm a mom of two little boys. How can I look after them? My home is in the country, but now, I can't even drive to get groceries. Life is not fair! I lost my dream career as a psychiatric nurse. A patient caused my injury, and I am in a brace from the waist up and can no longer use my right arm . . . and I'm right-handed! I have no family here. What do I do?"

I felt like my life was over. There were no smiles, no matter how deep I dug. Dad said, "Renee, I'm so sorry, but remember that you will never be given more than you can handle in life. You are a strong woman."

I knew If I chose not to give up, I would have a long road ahead. After some very teary and angry days, life was about to take a turn. I was alive and had two beautiful sons to look after. They deserved to see and feel their mom's love and smiles.

We sold the home and moved to the city so I could take the bus for groceries and the kids to school. And it was time for physiotherapy. It was amazing how I turned my smiles into a passion for helping myself and my children. I learned to write with my left hand (I couldn't even read my own notes). I completed a correspondence business diploma within nine months because I knew I could not be a nurse anymore. I was proud of myself, and I would beam with a smile.

How many people could say they were so fortunate to dig deep within themselves and find their inner strength to not give up and sparkle again.

Physiotherapy took almost a year. I finally could drive a car and have the arm strength to get a casserole out of the oven. My sons were young but most helpful and loving. Now that my sons are young men and have families of their own, I've often wondered if helping me is what made them so caring, loving, and hardworking?

I was fortunate my sister took me under her wing for one month, showing me the shortened Cole Notes version of her career. It was a tough choice. I needed the assistance to find a career, but she lived a fourteen-hour drive away, and I had to find someone to care for my children—just another part of the journey.

Fifteen months after the incident, my new career path started. Gratefully, I began as a rookie, and with my experience, I slowly grew as a business finance manager for almost twenty years. I poured my passion and sparkle into helping to meet others' needs on another level, from nursing to finance. In the finance field, I developed skills that would help me negotiate the best rates, which earned me a place of recognition for my service.

My shoulder never regained full movement and is now becoming arthritic as the years go on. I decided to do something different, still wanting to work and have ongoing interactions with others. So, I started a new journey studying for my real estate license.

I completed my real estate license! What an amazing occupation! I was able to bring all my passion and years of experience to assist people in finding their little place of real estate paradise, along with any finance questions they may have had. If my clients were on a budget, I was able to share renovation tips and ideas that looked incredible without breaking the bank. Many times, we just made a few adjustments, a tweak here and there, and that would have many people excited about reaching their new goals and accomplishments. Sometimes people just needed a little help picturing a brighter picture or an opportunity. My passion for others would always shine through with my smiles.

I'm now married to a wonderful man, John, and we have a blended family of four children and seven grandchildren. John has often commented how I always look at the best in people—sometimes to a fault. But, he loves me for it.

Sometimes people would say, "Oh, you poor thing! What that patient did to you." But, let me share with you that I'm so grateful that this test was part of my life journey. I do not want to ever think what my life would have been if I was not on this path. I've learned and grown so much, and I'm proud of the woman I have become, and I continue growing. I now know how to value myself, and I understand the boundaries of how we should accept treatment and how to treat others with respect and consideration.

Life is full of blessings. Sometimes, we just need to open our eyes. My passion now is life—the lives of others along with my life. I'm on a quest to read books and listen to audiobooks every day, sometimes, even when I'm sleeping, to see what I can learn.

I am now able to take my past education, experiences, and passion and become a business mentor and coach full-time. I have a worldwide online attraction marketing business. I work daily, assisting people from all over the world with their businesses. With technology, we now have the option to see each other face to face, study each other's body language, and hear others' voices in our business meetings via Zoom. We share and feel that smile that gives so many of us our strength and validation. I'm pursuing my life mission of being the best leader and supporting mentor I can be to assist others to grow and become the best they can possibly be. We need to be honest and real with our vulnerabilities and brave enough to go forward on our life journey. As I say to my children, life is full of lessons, some harder than others, but we get stronger with every challenge, and then, we move on to the next.

We never truly know what path our lives will take or who we will meet on our way. I just believe everything happens for a reason, even at times when we don't understand why. I'm truly blessed by my life experiences.

My smiles have always got me through good and rough patches. When people look sad or grumpy, their face works like a mirror. I like to smile at them with the hopes that I can change their day, and that enhances my day. It only takes seventeen muscles to smile and forty-three to frown. When I see people who smile, I always smile back, thinking, "I wonder what you are smiling about. What's your secret?" From my experiences, even when you may feel like you have hit a roadblock in life, laughter is definitely the best medicine.

Smile today, and see whose life you can touch.

Before I close my eyes each day, with my biggest smile, I always say what I'm the most grateful for—even the smallest thing.

BIOGRAPHY

Renee Robinson grew up as an underprivileged child in a small town on Vancouver Island. Since she was a child, she had programmed herself to be a people pleaser. As an adult, it's no surprise Renee graduated as a nurse with a special performance in psychology. With a passion for constantly learning, she later learned business, earned her real estate license, and started coaching leadership and business strategies to families and individuals around the world online. When not absorbed in one of her many new books, Renee enjoys learning to paddleboard and travel in her motorhome. When happily at home, she loves baking with the grandbabies, spending time with family, and meeting new people. She lives in British Columbia with her husband and extended family.

Connect with Renee Robinson via https://linktr.ee/businessoptions

CHAPTER 25

Focus Is The Catalyst

By Robert Peizer

"Focus: a constant central point of attention or activity."
"Catalyst: a change agent, something that causes results."

I have two stories of devastating loss and heartbreak, and how I learned to shift my focus from obstacles to opportunities and take my power back. I share them because, through my stories, I have helped many find their own inner strength and the ability to reshape their lives in service of their dreams. In doing so, I found my purpose and passion—helping people transform from victims to victors, focusing on opportunities rather than obstacles, and living their best lives.

1. The End of A Dream

I was training for the 1980 Olympics. I was a competitive springboard diver, something of a prodigy, trained by some of the world's best elite coaches. During high school, while others were dating, partying, vacationing—I stayed focused. Although I was blessed with enough brains to get a scholarship to a private school, I wasn't too keen on academics. I was focused on becoming the best diver I could be. My vision was big and pulled me forward: an Olympic gold medal.

I was undefeated for three years in my age group, high school champion, state champion, and Eastern Interscholastic champion. I was second in the YMCA Nationals at fifteen and placed twelfth in the US Open Nationals at sixteen. *I was focused; my willpower and self-control were aligned on a vision, and I was living my best life.*

During college, I took a rare break at Christmas and visited my parents in North Carolina. I went horseback riding, something I used to do with my sister when we were young. I was riding through the woods when a dog jumped out of the bushes and spooked the horse. In the next second, I was airborne, completely out of the saddle, and headed toward a large tree at the junction of two trails. I managed to turn myself sideways and struck the tree across both my thighs. I was lucky I didn't hit my head—but I hyperextended both legs, nearly breaking them, bending them both the wrong way, stretching, and tearing the tendons and ligaments of both knees.

I had to walk back a mile to the stables. My knees had swelled up nearly to the size of melons. I spent the next day in agony in the back seat of my parent's car, driving to Maryland to my cousin's wedding, at which I tried to dance with my relatives. It was agonizing.

I returned to school, but my heart wasn't in it. My legs were basically shot. I quit school, and I came home wondering what to do. My vision, my focus, my central point of action and activity no longer served me. **I was focusing on obstacles and not opportunities.** I struggled to find direction and meaning. I began to look at what had moved me to action previously in my life: How had I developed the willpower and self-control to become a world-class athlete?

"What you want is all downstream."
—Esther Hicks, *The Law of Attraction*

It was because what I had focused on—my vision—pulled me toward it and gave me energy. Sure, there were times when I had wanted to relax, let go, slack off a little, and just be a normal teenager. But my vision of what life would be like when I obtained my goal filled me with power. The joy and fulfillment I envisioned in winning the Olympics made the sacrifice along the way shrink to insignificance in comparison. *That goal was energetically downstream, aligned with my willpower, discipline, and self-control.*

"Always remember, your focus determines your reality."
—Jedi Knight Qui-Gon Jinn

At school, I studied languages (Chinese, Russian and Arabic) because I enjoyed them. That's not to say they didn't take a lot of effort, but it was not a struggle because I enjoyed them. When there is a focus, a vision, a central point of attention or activity that pulls you downstream toward it, *effort does not equal struggle*. Focused effort becomes self-control, and self-control becomes discipline. Discipline is "disciple-ship," which means keeping at something and pouring your energy into it. It comes from a *place of service to that thing,* being a disciple to it.

I found a unique graduate school offering a master's degree in international business that required proficiency in a foreign language. All I needed to do was *shift my focus* to a new vision, and I would begin a new life. My focus—my central point of attention and activity—pulled me downstream into a new future.

Meanwhile, the United States boycotted the 1980 Olympics in Russia because it invaded Afghanistan. *There would have been no Olympics for me in any case.* I realized life had taught me a lesson. I had been single-point focused on my diving career—but what would I have done after it ended? Diving is not like football or basketball—there is virtually no follow-up career, except coaching, after active participation in the sport. No disrespect to the honorable occupation of sports coaching—but was that what I wanted to do for the rest of my life? What kind of lifestyle would it provide me with? And what if I wanted to start a family? Could coaching be a future I could embrace forever? I saw I had a short-term focus, a myopic vision of what was possible for me.

What is a big enough vision for your life?

That's when I realized that **focus is catalytic—it causes manifestation**. Focus is a tool that **amplifies vision**. It **multiplies effort**. It can be brought to bear on anything.

Conscious focus is the most powerful tool humans have. We have the unique and extraordinary ability to imagine a result, an outcome, a vision—and the ability to narrow our attention and focus on what it will take to manifest that vision—**even if we don't see the entire picture, all the steps, all at once.**

I realized I had more power to choose my focus than I had ever thought possible. I had been focusing on the obstacles—my ruined knees, my lost vision—which left me powerless. And the obstacles expanded until they were all I could see. My **unconscious** focus caused me to experience depression. It was when I realized that I could **consciously** control my focus—shift it— that I regained my power and began a new life.

As I began my new life, I focused on personal development. I learned most of us use our focus backward; that is, we look at our past and project our future based on it, as if our future is **necessarily** controlled by what's happened in the past. **We focus on our conclusions** about the past, when they are simply the stories that we tell ourselves about events about which we know only one side—our own. **And we live as if these stories represent the only way things can be.** The hard reality is, there is nothing that makes our stories necessarily true but our sometimes-unconscious choices, our often-unplanned decision to think it so. In the end, we have literally made up our version of events— and that version controls our future.

It's the future we imagine (conscious focus) that creates how we feel about life. When we focus on something worthwhile we are imagining for ourselves (a vision), we become energized, excited, *spirited,* and passionate, then use willpower and discipline to manifest the vision. If we focus on obstacles, we become *dispirited*, lethargic, and depressed. We lose sight of what energizes us—a future that's exciting, interesting, stimulating—and focus on the obstacles, which grow and take our energy away. We have the ability to choose a new, more energizing focus at any time. The only limit is: *how conscious is the choice?* What is big enough, exciting enough, and fulfilling enough to deserve your focus? And what are the stories you focus on that are holding you back?

2. Heartbreak

As a result of learning to *consciously focus*, my life expanded by orders of magnitude. After graduating with a master's in international business, I traveled the world, became an entrepreneur and also a musician, performing in front of hundreds at musical festivals. I developed into a thought leader and coach, focused on catalyzing change and transforming lives.

I co-founded a biotech equipment design company and then shifted focus to become a marketing consultant for internet startups in Silicon Valley, where global titans like Apple, Amazon, and Google were starting their growth runs.

Then came 9/11. Months later, partly as a result of the devastating toll that horrific event took on our country, the stock market crash began. The Bay Area's economy tanked, and many people's finances were ruined. With another shift of focus, some colleagues and I formed a consulting company in the relatively new field of website security and digital signatures. We gained some international clients, which insulated us somewhat from the vagaries of the US economy. Conscious focus was serving me well.

As part of the expansion in my life, I became a percussionist specializing in African drumming, and this activity took me to many places. In November 2002, I participated in a large Day of The Dead procession in Tucson, Arizona. I met a woman who owned a cafe there. I fell in love with her, hard. Two months later, I sold everything and moved to Tucson from San Francisco, intending to go into the restaurant business at some point with her. I felt this was the biggest adventure of my life and I had met my soulmate. I could run my consulting business from my laptop and my phone; it didn't matter where I lived. I was ecstatic.

One day, about six months later, she said she was driving to Phoenix to visit her father. She had only been gone a few hours when she called me from the road. She said she was actually leaving me and wouldn't be back. She hung up, and I couldn't reach her again, no matter how I tried. I was devastated.

I fell into depression as hard as I had fallen in love. It didn't matter that I *knew* I was focusing on the loss, on the story that I had given my life to her and she threw it away. My story was too loud, too persistent. I *lived* the story that I had given her everything—and she didn't want it.

I couldn't hear anything else—**for four years**. I lived the story of loss and despair every minute of that time.

It wasn't until I remembered a personal development course I had taken, one that transformed my understanding of how we develop and then maintain our stories forever unless we realize we can step outside them long enough to **shift our focus**, that I began my recovery. Someone had asked me, "How long are you willing to keep paying the price of living in the past? What is it costing you?" That question—and the answer—catalyzed my life.

The other part of that training focused on making a difference in other people's lives. I reconnected with that community and spent the next five years training myself in contributing to benefit others' lives.

I learned in the most profound way that sharing myself, especially the vulnerabilities and shortcomings, had the most impact on people's lives. I learned my purpose was to grow that ability to **share and say things that make a difference.**

The more I gave, the more I got.

I became a public speaker who contributed to thousands through transformational leadership. When I learned to consciously focus on a future that energizes rather than the past that depletes, it freed up my life, and I saw I could share that idea with others and make a difference in their lives.

With conscious focus, I *freed the emotional energy that enlarged my vision*. I saw how much of my prior focus had been on me: my obstacles, my reasons, my excuses: me, me, me. When I turned my focus outward and dreamed bigger, I saw that touching, moving, and inspiring others gave me energy rather than taking it. The more I focused on helping others, the more energy, resources, and freedom I had.

I became a catalyst, a change agent, for people to fulfill their vision—and, in so doing, I found my purpose, passion, and fulfillment.

BIOGRAPHY

Robert Peizer is a successful entrepreneur, life coach, musician and writer. He has a master's degree in international business from the top-ranked Thunderbird School of Global Management, speaks Mandarin Chinese, and has traveled throughout China, Taiwan, and Europe. While living in the Bay Area, he co-founded and managed several companies, and also found a passion for percussion, studying and playing with professional African musicians from Guinea, Mali, and the Congo. He found his life's purpose after coursework with the Dale Carnegie Institute, Steven Covey, Tony Robbins, Landmark Education, and The Total Integration Institute, when he saw the impact of helping people shift their thoughts, words, and actions to access their innate and unique powers, and catalyze them into action and fulfillment. His decades of business management, thought leadership and personal development, along with elite athletic training in his early years, form the basis for his multifaceted consulting practice.

Contact Robert Peizer via https://linktr.ee/robertpeizer

CHAPTER 26

Gratitude, Grace, Grit

By Ronelle Brown

Like many, I've experienced the highs of hope and the lows of loss. I write about both to encourage others to (1) live life fully from day one till day done, and (2) see overcoming as the key to becoming whole.

To understand my story, it's necessary to know that my husband and I emigrated from South Africa in our late twenties. What we experienced there, in the seventies, eighties, and nineties, taught us about privilege, opportunity, responsibility, freedom, and forgiveness. I am grateful for those lessons.

It was three years into our marriage that Paul and I relocated to the USA. We intended to be there for three years to help companies fix the Y2K computer bug. But after 9/11, we knew we needed to go all in.

We worked hard to make the most of all the opportunities that we were privileged to pursue, including becoming permanent residents and then US citizens. It wasn't easy starting over in our thirties, but we knew we had to put down roots. What made it easier was friendships and finding our passions.

My husband and I worked in the same department of the same company in Milwaukee. There, we met two other South African families who had immigrated around the same time as us. We shared common backgrounds and shared new experiences. The Oliver and Peirce families became our beloved, chosen family for almost fifteen years. We spent all the holidays together and watched their kids grow.

It was in 2012 that the three South African husbands and buddies—Paul, Tony, and Clinton— discovered that they could do a team triathlon together. Their first race became "legendary," and soon, Paul and Tony had set their sights on becoming Ironmen. I started running half marathons to "keep up."

We had traveled regularly for a few years but put that on hold when Paul was given several challenging leadership assignments and also sent on a leadership rotation to Baltimore for six months. After he returned, Paul was given a confidential assignment he could not discuss with me. He worked round the clock on what I later learned was a strategic merger and acquisition. I was so proud of him.

I invested the time when Paul was away to challenge myself to get fit and develop my self-belief. I now look back at the months that I spent alone as truly lifesaving. I needed to know I could do life alone.

But life was busy. So, we put off many good things, including visiting our families in South Africa. I regret that because, while we had a sense of accomplishment, family and friends spell love T-I-M-E.

Paul was tired; he shared that he did not want to keep sacrificing personal time for professional prestige and promotion. So, we started planning our twentieth-anniversary trip. But we never got there.

Saturday, June 6, 2015, the first day of Wisconsin Bike Week, was planned to be a fun-filled day. Paul and Tony had a training ride in the morning on a route they often rode for their Ironman Wisconsin preparations. Then, Paul intended to leave Tony to do a long run while he cycled back alone to go to a doctor's appointment with me. Next, we would all meet at the Peirce household to help celebrate their son's high school graduation with a barbecue with all his friends. Afterward, Paul planned to nap before having dinner with buddies from Baltimore. It was supposed to be a busy Saturday in a very good way.

Only it wasn't.

My first clue that something was wrong came when I checked on Paul's progress before going on my morning run. He had asked me to run nearby just in case he got a flat tire. Paul's FindMyPhone dot showed he was five miles away, so I expected to see him arrive home before I finished my shortened run. But I didn't. Growing concerned, I checked my phone again. Paul's dot appeared to be in the same place. He didn't answer when I tried to call. I checked the network and tried again. No answer. Had Paul tried to call me? I was afraid he'd be angry with me. So, I began driving to where the FindMyPhone dot said Paul was, thinking he had suffered a flat tire and was waiting for me. I was not ready for what I saw.

The road was blocked off at the intersection just before where I expected to find Paul. I tried to talk myself into driving up to the officer directing traffic to the detour, but I was too afraid of what she might say. So, I studied my phone and convinced myself the dot was further away and that Paul was stuck on the other side. I tried to call again. No answer. I tried Tony, hoping he could tell me what exact route they had ridden. I knew Tony might not be able to answer but prayed that he would. He didn't.

I was panicking, but then my sister called me from South Africa. She suggested I go home to leave Paul a note in case he arrived home via a detour and worried about me. It was the hope and distraction that I needed. I drove home, praying all the way that Paul was already home waiting for me.

I remember how I stood in our empty garage calling Paul and Tony's phones repeatedly, hoping and praying that Tony would answer and tell me Paul was with him. Finally, I got back in my car to drive the five miles back to the intersection where I needed to ask an unthinkable question. I never got there.

I was two miles away when my phone rang, and the caller ID said it was the Muskego Police Department. My heart plummeted. They asked where I was, and I told them I had pulled off to the side of the road as I was looking for my husband, who was late. Then I asked if Paul was okay. They said they were trying to figure that out. They were at our home and needed my help. They asked if they could come to me, but I said it was easier if I drove home. I prayed all the way home: "Wake Up! Wake Up!"

I'll never forget how I felt coming around the corner to see the police car parked outside our house. I'll never forget how professionally and gently they introduced themselves and asked about my identity. And I'll never forget the physical pain I felt when I heard them say that they were investigating a motor vehicle versus bicycle incident that had resulted in two cyclist fatalities. I remember saying, "Not Tony, too!" and the two officers' expressions changed. They had not yet identified them both.

Until that point, I assumed that Paul was on his way home alone. It had never occurred to me that Paul and Tony had been struck and killed together less than fifteen minutes after leaving our house.

Later, we learned that Paul and Tony had died at the exact same moment. They were struck from behind by a car that drifted into the emergency lane and hit them at full speed, going 55 miles per hour. Witnesses saw the young man driving with his eyes closed and then hit them. Two of the witnesses were off-duty first responders, so Paul and Tony received CPR in seconds, but their injuries were too severe. The young man and his two friends were in shock as they called 9-11 for them.

At age forty-five, my husband Paul's life ended suddenly and tragically. Paul had been run over. His body had been broken, and he died in a ditch. His best friend, Anthony (fifty-four), died next to him.

Nothing prepares you for something like this. I could tell you about the rest of the day in detail. It's burned into my memory. But I don't want to be seen as one of the victims. I am one of the survivors, along with Tony's wife and children, Paul's parents, our family, and Paul and Tony's many friends, especially the Peirces and Kadlecs. We are united by tragedy and so blessed to have loved them.

So why tell this story? I hope that anyone reading this will take something from it that they need. If you are someone who has been making decisions that could endanger lives, then I hope you'll find the courage to act differently. If you are someone who has been taking things for granted or putting off important things, then I hope that you will embrace today and live more joyfully and gratefully. Or, if you are someone who wishes that something like this never happens in your family, then I hope that you can believe that, even if it does, you can and must go on. If we did, so can you.

What I hope to communicate are survivor's lessons that I've learned over the last seven years. Looking back, I believe there were three key attitudes that helped us slowly survive, strive, and thrive.

1.   Start with Gratitude for what we still GET to give and receive.

2.   Give ourselves and others Grace and time to grieve and grow.

3.   Let Grit grow in us and become our fuel (so that we become stronger and more resilient).

Gratitude is what I had to deliberately feel for my heart to go on. First, I clung to the belief that my husband did and would always love me, that he was proud of me, and that I would never walk alone. Then, I cherished every kind word, every act of compassion, and each time that someone said his name.

Grace is what I tried to give myself and others. I became acutely aware of how easy it was to lash out over little controllable things. I chose to embrace solitude in order to spare others unintended hurt. And I worked on forgiving the unforgivable. I worked to face my grief and let go of any timetables.

Grit is what I needed to use to do the hard things alone that I had left to do. But not all of them, and not at once. I tried to keep moving, mostly forward, to feel connected to the life I'd lost.

What I did that kept me going during Year 1 was training for a triathlon in memory of Paul and Tony. The long hours of training, both alone and with my friend, Lettie (Tony's widow), were a great way for us to grieve with grace, grit, and gratitude. We both had our focus on a goal that our husbands challenged us to accomplish. And we did it together, on June 5, 2016, with our closest friends cheering us both on.

The next day, on the first anniversary of their last ride together, Lettie and I put our first two triathlon medals around two white crosses by the roadside. Our husbands, Paul and Tony, had finished their races together. Lettie and I had started our new races together. We had forged unbreakable bonds of grief, grace, grit, and gratitude. Together, we celebrated the strength that our husbands had instilled in us by accomplishing a goal greater than ourselves that proved to us we could still rise.

As we walked away, I thought back to how I got my medal with Paul's date of birth on my chest. It had been "randomly" assigned as my first triathlon's race number. It was not the first time that I had seen a sign like that. I lifted up my head and smiled because Paul always said, "You'll never walk alone." I don't. None of us do. That's why I share this story. I want to share my scars and my hope with others.

Finally, you may be wondering what you're able to take from this chapter that can serve you or the teams you lead. Here are two possibilities: (1) Ask someone who is grieving a loss what they know now about *legacy*, and (2) prepare now for the day when either you are a widow or leave one behind.

BIOGRAPHY

Ronelle Brown's story started in South Africa, moved to the USA, and is still being written. Today, she applies her decades of project and team management experience to help people start and scale global businesses. Ronelle honors her husband Paul's spirit by pursuing a life of passion and purpose. She reminds herself daily, "Life is a gift with no guarantees. Give it all you've got!"

Connect with Ronelle Brown via https://linktr.ee/ronellebrown

CHAPTER 27

The Rebel Approach

By Scott Lewis

My work life started early, growing up on a cotton farm in the plains of West Texas. I learned the value of hard work from an early age. I also knew, very early, that I didn't want to do that for the rest of my life. I always had this crazy tug inside of me, the almost unfillable void to experience anything and everything this world had to offer. And I was struck with this crazy notion that I could do anything that I set my mind to. That internal confidence also led to many crazy roads: some great, some not so great. I would define my journey as the "Rebel Approach" as my biggest fear—a sheer terror really—was that of working a job, being controlled by a boss, and being told what to do. I hated it. That option scared the hell out of me! And I would say it was that fear that led to the rebel inside. I would say I wasn't a rebel in a way you might be thinking. My Rebel Approach to business and the thought that I could truly do anything that I set my mind to set me on a life course of the entrepreneur. Too many lessons to count. Success and failure— truly blood and guts. But it was the most rewarding life I could ever imagine, filled with the thrill of victory and the agony of defeat. Being a serial entrepreneur for my entire life, I have many stories of success and failure and more life lessons than I could ever count. But one story comes to mind! Through this story, I would like to share with you what

I believe are some of the most important life lessons I have learned along the way.

This true and crazy story took place in The Woodlands, TX, in the fall of 1994. And like any good story, this experience was a real gift; it was a lesson I needed to learn.

When I was twenty-nine years old (I am fifty-six now), I sold a business, and I invested everything I had in an exotic animal game park in Houston, TX. It was 300 acres of tropical paradise with a large beautiful crystal-clear lake in the center. We had imported exotic animals from all seven continents: lions, tigers, leopards, hippos, rhinos, giraffes, monkeys, various African and Asian hoofed stock, and probably seventy-five different breeds of deer and antelope. It was located outside Houston, right on the edge of the San Jacinto River. It was a magical destination.

There were several million dollars' worth of animals, including 100 ostriches, which were worth $50,000 each at the time (that's another story in itself). I invested all the money I had in this park and the animals.

It was September of 1994, and it rained all weekend long, and Houston was flooding. On Monday, I headed out to the park, and it was still raining. When I made the turn on the interstate, I realized the property was being flooded, and about half of it was underwater during that time. The animals had been forced into the smaller, higher elevation areas. It again rained all day with torrential downpours, and even though we were informed that we were way above the 100-year floodplain, it rained approximately twenty-three inches over twenty-four hours. The river authority panicked, and they opened the floodgates.

So then, within just a few hours, we had another fifteen feet of water on the property. Almost the entire park was underwater. Most of the animals were drowning or floating down the river. It was just horrible. Heartbreaking. I loved these animals so much, and the suffering was immense. Obviously, people were also being affected, and so our first priority was to help as many of our neighbors as possible. Our buddy had boats, and we began rescuing people. I fished one little girl out of the water by her hair and pulled her into the boat. It was devastating. I was interviewed by CNN and all the major channels, and the images are forever burned in my heart.

We lost almost all of our animals. It was a horrific event, and it greatly affected me. Not only did it affect me financially, but to see, witness, and feel that sort of devastation and suffering was too much.

As the water started coming down, I was in touch with a guy named Cash Wiley. Cash had a group of guys who were rodeo cowboys—really tough guys (you might call them Rebels)—and they went around the country trapping and relocating animals. That's how they make their living. They were friends of ours since we got a lot of our animals from them. They stayed with us when they saw this event and assisted us and others during the flood. They saved many lives with their heroic actions.

After the storm had subsided, we went out to see what was left and secured any animals that had crossed the highway. Some animals had crossed the road, so we were able to save a herd of red lechwe, which are beautiful, exotic, red antelopes from Africa. The whole family had made it across the road. It was a miracle. They were saved.

There was a dike in the middle of the property, and we found King, a huge bull elk standing knee-deep in water, still as a statue. The water subsided, so he was up to about his knees. We figure he had been standing there for three days. Cash Wiley, his crew, my partner, and I came up with a strategy to rescue King. We got a boat, and the plan was to tranquilize him, put him in the boat and then take him to safety. Crazy idea, right?

The six of us went out in this boat, and we got about 100 feet from the elk, and Cash shot the elk with the tranquilizer gun. As you can imagine, it startled and scared him. We did not think ahead. King jumped into the water and started swimming towards a huge high fence that had been collecting all the trash. The debris was all floating on top of the water, and it was covered in logs, moss, and all sorts of garbage. King started swimming in all that. You could see his head and massive antlers.

I looked around in almost a shock-like state, and two of Cash's partners jumped into the water to go after this elk. I was looking at that water, thinking there was no way in hell I was getting in there. There were snakes and all sorts of danger and nastiness in that water.

Anyway, they were swimming after King, and I was sitting there thinking there was no way I'd get into this water, right? I mean, it's just not going to happen.

There were jet skis and paddle boats from our lake lodged in the trees—just all kinds of trash, debris, and equipment. We were surrounded by stuff. Then, out of the corner of my eye, I saw what I thought was just a large tree branch. Something to grab hold of a sense of security! I reached up and grabbed the branch. It broke and fell in the middle of the boat. I quickly realized my hand was on fire. What I thought was a big branch was actually a pretty small branch covered in millions of fire ants.

As soon as the branch fell, the entire bottom of the boat was covered in millions of fire ants. Without much thought, suddenly, the water didn't look so bad! My hands were on fire! I can still remember the pain; there were ants everywhere. I immediately had a whole new perspective on the situation and the water. So, I immediately jumped into the water with all the trash and everything else in a desperate attempt to get the fire ants off me. What a relief.

We had to use buckets to fill the boat with enough water to float all the fire ants out so we could get back on the boat. Then, we had to pull it while dog-paddling to a place where we could start it back up and get out of there. King, like so many other animals, didn't make it.

This tragedy holds such a powerful message. I have relived it many times over. From this experience and tragedy, I have gained a whole new perspective on life and perception versus reality.

Don't put things off. Don't wait until it is too late. See the danger before your life (or livelihood) is at stake. Don't let the toxic environment force you to act out of desperation.

When an industry is being disrupted, there are obviously a lot of cowboys—Rebels—out there. Those are the people of the Wild, Wild West. They look for opportunities, and they're not scared because all they see is the gold, the target (in this case, the elk). For me, all I could see was the trash, the snakes, and everything else surrounding the water because the boat seemed very safe. But suddenly, when fire ants took over the boat, the boat became deadly. The fire ants are the final stage of disruption. Once we have fire ants in our boat, we decide that we've got to jump into the water just like everybody else. In that environment, only the strongest will survive. For most folks, that means it's too late.

You have many decisions in front of you, but how many true opportunities to change the course of your life, to set a new sail to define your legacy? Most of us are willing to sit back and watch the disruption until it's too late, when in fact, that's where the gold is. I always say in business, fortune is made in the mess. In order to create the desired outcome, which, for most, is time and money freedom, you must disrupt something. Look at everything from the Rebel Approach. Turn it upside down; create a mess that will solve the problem. Most successful people I know are not afraid of getting wet or messy. You will fail. You will fall, and it might be painful. And through all that, you will build your story— your *legacy*. Don't wait until there are fire ants in your boat. How long will you wait to make the jump?

The one thing that I have learned from building multiple companies from the ground up and being a lifetime entrepreneur is that the most valuable thing in the world is when you can impact someone else's life—truly add real value! I have seen that most people never get on the right boat or are afraid to jump off that hamster wheel and take a chance at financial freedom. As my friend, Rob Flicks, says, "Once people get a taste of financial freedom, time freedom, and money freedom, they will fight through iron walls to keep it!" I believe that is true for me. My motto is, "Do *what* you want, *when* you want, *where* you want, with *who* you want." What do you want? Try the Rebel Approach.

BIOGRAPHY

Scott Lewis is a passionate visionary, and his legacy is inspiring entrepreneurs to go "All In," conquer their internal battles, and win in their quest for success. Scott adopted his unwavering desire for financial freedom from his mentor, Zig Ziglar, and his belief that if you help enough people get what they want, you will ultimately get what you want. He has been an entrepreneur since launching his first business at the age of nineteen while attending Texas Tech University. As CEO of UniCorp Marketing, Scott lived his passion for golf while marketing for companies like GM, AT&T, and others on the PGA Golf Tour. Scott has carried a single-digit handicap for years. He's the founding father of Sunjoi Corporation, a manufacturing and marketing company of unique outdoor living products lines sold in national retail chains. He's co-founder of Whispering Eye Tequila and even owned an exotic animal park. Owning one of the largest Century 21 franchises in the USA led Scott to his love of real estate and his current passion of building a team of thousands of real estate agents globally while inspiring them to be champions!

Connect with Scott Lewis via https://linktr.ee/ScottLewis

CHAPTER 28

The Power of Being Wrapped In Love

By Tansy Serediak

I have always had a deep desire to become a mom. From an early age, I would have a baby doll in my arms or push my doll in a toy stroller. I brought my "baby" with me everywhere; she was buckled in the car seat next to me wherever we'd go. As I grew up, I loved babysitting the neighborhood kids. Children bring so much joy into our lives! An unconditional love. I wanted at least five children of my own!

In the early morning of February 24, 2003, no cry rang out in my hospital room. I had just labored for eight hours without any pain medication and epidural; I felt every second of this birth. The instant my son was born, every ounce of excruciating pain had vanished. The most wonderful feeling of love flooded my body. I was a parent again—to my second child!

At that moment I became aware of the silence; I didn't hear a thing. 'That's odd,' I thought. I should have been holding my baby by now. I looked over to find the nursing staff and the doctor standing around my baby, just looking at him. I looked at my then-husband, who was holding my hand, and our world fell apart at that moment.

The doctor on call at the time came to my bedside and asked me in his next breath, "Couldn't you tell?" I was beyond confused by his question. "Couldn't I tell what?" I asked. "That your son was dead. Couldn't you feel that he wasn't moving?" I felt the rawest form of fear I had ever felt; darkness enveloped me.

You know the darkness that suffocates you, the one that makes the very act of breathing impossible? I was so deep in the belly of darkness; I didn't know how to escape. Come to think of it, I wanted to just stay there. It was easier than facing anything else around me or, heaven forbid, any emotion that might well up. I was numb, and the tears were streaming. Little did I know that they would continue to flow every day for the next six months.

I started questioning myself and began analyzing, in detail, the activities of my last day of the pregnancy. I actually didn't feel him moving very much. You see, I was forty-two weeks pregnant. I had carried this active baby to term. Just a week before, I was listening to his heartbeat in my doctor's office during our checkup. Everything was perfect! My doctor told me that things start slowing down during the last weeks: that the baby would be "settling in" for his arrival, and less movement was normal! So, I didn't think anything of it. Oh my God, I should have noticed. Why didn't I notice? This was all my fault. I felt shame and guilt. Was there something wrong with my instincts? How did I miss this? 'I'm a terrible person, and I don't deserve to be a parent,' my mind reeled.

The staff had shut the curtains and dimmed the lights in the room (because more darkness would help somehow?). I remember my parents entering the room; my in-laws brought my then two-year-old daughter, who didn't understand what was going on. People were talking in a hushed manner, and all I could do was lay there. Their voices sounded muffled and unclear like I was inside a glass bottle, and no sound was quite clear enough to hear.

Later, I was transferred to a private room down the hall. A nurse brought my stillborn baby to me. For the first time, I cradled that sweet boy to my chest, all wrapped in a knitted blanket of blue. I felt all the love while my now vanishing hopes and dreams for his future washed over me. How did this happen? Why was this happening to me? In that cascading moment, there was a ray of sunshine. The brightest, most radiant light, a linear beam from the space in the window where the curtains split open, directly over that beautiful baby in my arms. I froze. It felt like I was being wrapped in a blanket of heavenly, healing love—a love with which only God could fill us. I took ten seconds and mentally froze this picture onto my heart. This was the moment that would be etched into my very soul—to remember for my entire lifetime. An image that I return to whenever I think of him. Pure Love.

In the stillness of that moment, I heard a voice. It came from deep within. It told me to see the love all around me, to hold onto the light, and that the light would always guide me through the darkness. For the first time in twenty-four hours, I felt a sense of calmness that I had never felt before.

I held my baby for the next two hours, just staring at his face. It looked like he was sleeping. Just peacefully sleeping. 'Is this real?' I thought. I prayed that I could just push pause, right here, right now, and savor this moment forever. Little did I know, the difficult part was yet to come. The real loss would begin then. The nurse came to my room and gently told me that it was time to take my baby away. I don't envy their job, and I'm not sure I would personally be able to do it. I honestly didn't know if I could pass my baby to her, knowing it was the last time I would ever hold him. I couldn't. My mom, who had come in, talked me through passing him to her, so she could be the one to take that burden. I will forever be thankful to her for helping me in that way. She has been an instrumental support to me my whole life. She saved me from that trauma.

After losing Connor, I was faced with planning a funeral. A local family-owned funeral home came into the hospital the day after I had lost him and donated their services as far as preparing him for burial and gifting us the smallest coffin I'd ever seen. Their grace and sympathy forever changed me. Truly, there are angels among us.

The tears were constantly melting my heart. I felt betrayed by my very body, which continued the natural process of lactating. 'Shouldn't our bodies know that after a baby dies, there is no one to nourish?' I thought while applying cabbage leaves to my breasts, and the tears came again.

A week went by in a blur, days melting into nights, over and over again. The world kept moving, even though I was frozen in time. The day of Connor's funeral came, and I awoke in a haze like I had every day for the past week. Pulling it all together, I reminded myself that if I just keep moving through the motions of the day, it would be over soon. The service was beautiful. What I remembered most was the glorious music. I couldn't tell you what the choir sang; I just remember thinking it sounded "heaven-sent." I have a recording of the entire service; I've never listened to it, not once in seventeen years. To me, it's not the words that were said or sang; it was the feeling of LOVE I remember most. A love that wrapped me up and held my broken pieces together.

Looking back at this time in my life, I realize how far I've come. I'm better able to analyze my emotions with the distance that time provided. Life has thrown me so many curveballs: so much joy and an equal amount of sorrow. Two years after Connor's death, I gave birth to identical twin boys. My daughter now had two brothers. My prayers had truly been answered. I now believe that Connor made room for those two babies to enter into my life. You see, at the time, Connor was going to be my last.

There was still so much pain between my husband and me. I healed in my own way, and he in his. Years later, our marriage fell apart. We just didn't have the tools to heal together. Loss, once again. A monumental shift was once again taking place in my life: another opportunity for growth. Then, I recalled the image that I had committed to my memory after my loss of Connor. I remembered the light. In a world where I felt alone once again, I simply imagined a healing light around my ex. Even though I was hurting, I sent him Love. This allowed me to establish healing of my own and a feeling of making a difference for him. We've managed to remain close through the years and raise our kids together in the spirit of joy and friendship.

This giving and receiving of love energy throughout my life has not only brought the addition of twins but a new husband. A man more in alignment with my energy than I ever thought possible. Goodness in our own lives is ultimately created by putting out goodness and love into the universe. I've learned that when we harness the ability to quiet our minds, the ongoing and endless thoughts still overwhelm our senses. We gain a sense of clarity that allows us to receive messages and healing that guides us. This enables us to become a more authentic, enlightened version of ourselves.

In continuing to rebuild my life beyond hurt, I experienced the proverbial "one step forward and two steps back." The day came when I would lose my job. My goodness! Just when you think things couldn't get any worse. There it was again: Loss, my old friend, was at the door. It was a shocking loss of security. I had worked for my family business and never thought in a million years that I would ever have to face the loss of employment. I loved what I did. So how then did I end up again, flat on my face? I worked faithfully for the company and celebrated and worked toward its growth for the past twenty-five years. I believe I held an integral part *in* that growth.

Growth. . . . A plan, continually evolving in my life. Like a child developing in the womb, I remind myself daily that the root of strength, healing, passion, and the ability to help others is found in the intricate pattern of LOVE. I have always desired to help people on their journey. Life is messy and never on a straight path. So, I ask myself: What can I do today to help someone navigate their path with the support and love of those who understand the feeling of the fall and rise? We can conquer anything together.

Love lingers in the light. It weaves a web connecting all of us in its infinite and boundless energy. It spans across time and space, offering us a guide, a purpose, a sign, healing, and a hand that will never let us go.

No matter what life throws our way, as crushing or as liberating as life is, healing can always be found wrapped in LOVE.

BIOGRAPHY

Tansy Serediak is a full-time wife and mother to three wonderful teens! A former executive officer of a manufacturing business that wasn't fulfilling her personal creative spark, she leaped out of her comfort zone and into a life of deeper satisfaction by writing, inspiring, and connecting with new people. Her creative writing has inspired her to tell her story, with the hope of sharing a healing journey, in the spirit of love after loss, with anyone who's walked a similar experience. Like a child developing in the womb, Tansy daily reminds herself that the root of strength, healing, passion, and the ability to help others, is found in the intricate pattern of LOVE.

Contact Tansy Serediak via https://linktr.ee/TansySerediak

CHAPTER 29

Hanging On Faith

By Venice Hughes

"Life" is a word with multiple definitions and experiences. Above all, life is not just about living but also about how a person determines that existence. Life is not the same for everyone. Hence, it is important to see that life, from a single point of view, is not fair. Life is a living adventure. We are living, we are leading our lives, and we are dying. By doing so, we strive to give order to our life.

Some people face several issues throughout their lives, while others do not. In one way, it is experienced by those who face no trouble in life. Most individuals who struggle in life look at situations in a certain way. Life is a precious asset that is sometimes taken for granted by individuals. Life is riddled with roads. Picking ones that are right is all you need to do.

Faith is an endeavor demonstrated day by day by our desire to believe that what God has guaranteed has been accomplished so far. Faith can be portrayed as living life quickly. Faith sees God's guarantees coming to fulfillment in progress; it may be a sure conviction that surpasses human comprehension. To me, faith is the understanding that even though good or bad things happen, God will always be there in all of His splendor. Faith waits patiently when it seems like there is no end. Faith, though keeping a thankful attitude, focuses on the positive. Faith may be as easy as understanding that you are not alone when humanity seems to have abandoned you.

I need to recognize that I'm walking on the right path, which is a far more appropriate target than what I and others would predict. Life has many twists and turns. In my situation, I was born with a heart defect: a narrowing of the pulmonary outflow tract that prevents blood flow from the right ventricle to the pulmonary ventricle. I've always had to be very selective in what I do so as not to overexert or stress myself out. My family always told me to take it easy, but I neglected them as a child that would not raise an alarm. Over the years, by using prayer to help me overcome this challenge, I have learned to cope with this condition. I grew up with my mother, my grandmother, and my two brothers. Every Sunday, my older brother and grandmother took me to church. That was a vital part of my family life. So, I heard about God as a kid and learned many of the stories in the Bible. But I didn't understand what they meant at the time. I felt, for some reason, I had to be "good" to go to heaven.

As I approached adulthood, my faith played a role in my life. My faith was what I relied on because knowing that God would deliver me through situations has been the reason I have had the endurance and strength to make it thus far. I do not understand His reasons, but my faith helped me recognize that I had to trust Him. It is understood that good results in life will far outweigh challenging trials. It is said that, no matter what, I must hold true that God is never far away from me or unable to console me.

Being faithful means doing whatever it takes for what you want, being steady while you're trying, and always do your best. I assume that without this virtue, no one would be able to do the things that they aim for most. With my faith, I look up to many people in my life, and there are many role models for me; but my mom is one in particular. Not only is she my mother, but she is my role model in life and faith. Her daily life sets an example for me.

My mother has taught me so much compared to people who do not know Jesus yet. Proverbs 31:10 states, "Who can find a virtuous woman? For her price is far above rubies."[22] My mother's love is truly priceless. She is the heart of the family and the glue that holds it together. My mother, a virtuous woman, has taught her family the ways of the Father in heaven and nurtured the family with the love of Christ. My mother disciplined us with care, wisdom, and trained my brother, sister, and me in the way we should go. As it states in Proverbs 22:6, "Train up a child in the way he should go: and when he is old, he will not depart from it."[23] So I thank my mother for the person she is.

There will, without any doubt, be moments where there is no faith. Doubt creeps into all facets of life and gradually transforms the very heart of life. When it comes to the state of my heart, I take it as both a challenge and a blessing. The burden is that in such situations, I have this condition that I have to deal with and the blessing that I can offer some hope. There needs to be a starting point on how we all began because it's difficult for life to just happen. Giving birth is a miracle, but with complications. When I was having my son, he got detached from me, and his heart rate dropped so low that I needed an emergency C-section. I was scared for my life and his because I did know if either or both of us would survive. My mother was with me at the time, and I saw that she was already praying. The doctors rolled me into the operating room and gave me an injection to knock me out, and then I had my son. I did not get to see him until sometime later.

My son is a blessing because one in every 100 births are detached from the mother. I thank God every day for sparing his life and mine. If either of us did not make it, it would be okay. I believe God is in

---

22   Prv 31:10 KJV
23   Prv 22:6 KJV

control of everything and is constantly testing my faith at every turn. I am a blessed person. Having belief in myself also means overcoming whatever I am facing, be it fears, life goals, or anything for that matter. It also means overcoming obstacles and trials as they come my way. My mother always urged me to believe in myself and put my mind at ease with the guidance of God. Whatever be the situation that comes my way, I first pray to God in order to be led in the right direction. I find it easier to look for answers to my issues having faith to rely on. It strengthens my thought processes as I realize that there is a way out, and I just need to think harder in order to get to it.

I believe that no matter how long God has given us to live our lives, life is God's gift. So we have to appreciate every minute we have in this world because tomorrow is not guaranteed. With faith, life is filled. No matter what, this concept of having total faith in someone or something comprises everything you do. Faith will still be there, whether it's with aspirations, God, family, relationships, or sports. It gives me meaning and my entire outlook on life is decided. My life would be boring and filled with emptiness without it. Having faith in my life adds so much to it. Faith is what held me together regardless of my struggles when I was about to fall apart. If I believed that all will be right again in the future, it gave me the power I needed to survive through today.

Faith is an important component of my life. Faith means trusting in other individuals and, most importantly, in myself. It will lead me through bad times and encourage you to find the meaning of my life.

It is possible to take your dream job and turn it into a reality. It is possible to have thought about something you want to do, something you want to build for yourself, be your own boss, and make it possible. Three years ago, I started working on my personal development. In this process, I concentrated on my own needs, ambitions, and the continuous acquisition of new knowledge in order to achieve them. My self-assessment represents a stable future. Life is a learning experience, and it will help me become a stronger person in everything I want to do, to be able to recognize my own strengths and weaknesses, whether it is positive skills and abilities that will help me to achieve or negative personal areas that need improvement, or what I have learned in order to help other people achieve their goals. Personal development not only focuses on important things in my life but also helps to handle critical situations. It helps me to connect with positive people. Having positive people around me motivates me to move forward. Personal development is hard work, and it takes consistency, patience, and time. It helps to improve my knowledge and helps to improve my life.

I started a new business endeavor. I was all in. I had faith in my ability to be successful. I had many "no's." I started having doubts and second-guessing myself, 'Could I do this?' I went to a training session that helped me get back on track and understand why I was doing this. The reason why I was doing this was for my family, as well as myself, to have freedom, fun, and fulfillment. After the training, a week later, I had success in enrolling many customers and hitting a few of the ranks. I had ups and downs but never quit because winners never quit and quitters never win. I had faith that everything would work. It is important that you believe in yourself, that self-confidence is good for your well-being, and that you are inspired to achieve your objectives. It is the accomplishment of goals that allow you to advance in life while enjoying happiness and achievement.

Faith determines how you view life. With it, your entire perspective on life can be optimistic. But without it, your view will be clouded with negativity. Faith helps you accomplish every objective that you put your mind to. You can do it if you believe that you can accomplish something.

As Martin Luther King Jr. said: "If you can't fly, then run, if you can't run then walk, if you can't walk then crawl, but whatever you do, you have to keep moving forward."[24] In your life, there will be numerous moments when you feel down and want to give up. The voice in your head is going to tell you to stop, and you will begin to doubt yourself. Never listen to that voice.

It takes faith in all facets of life. People can learn various skills, have experiences, and do the work cut out for them, but may end up struggling to accomplish the ultimate objectives of life without faith. It is a journey accomplished by, among others, overcoming defeat, resistance, obstacles, and laziness. All is possible with one's confidence.

If you don't believe in yourself, then honestly trusting in something else that you can't see, touch, feel, or physically behold would be difficult. I will make it, maybe not now, but absolutely and definitely in the time to come.

BIOGRAPHY

Venice Hughes is a Network Marketing Entrepreneur and works in the education industry. She is passionate about helping others succeed and to inspire and impact their lives. She is always reading books, whether on the phone, Kindle, or a hard copy. She has a vision to build others up to have a life of purpose. She believes that with one's faith, everything is achievable.

Contact Venice Hughes via https://linktr.ee/VeniceHughes_45

---

24 "If You Can't Fly, Then Run - Meaning and Usage," Literary Devices, September 10, 2017, https://literarydevices.net/if-you-cant-fly-then-run/.

The End